TRIUMPH
IN AUSTRALIA

TRIUMPH IN AUSTRALIA
MIKE GATTING'S 1986–87 CRICKET DIARY

MIKE GATTING

Macdonald
Queen Anne Press

A Queen Anne Press Book

© Mike Gatting 1987

First published in Great Britain in 1987 by
Queen Anne Press, a division of
Macdonald & Co (Publishers) Ltd
3rd Floor
Greater London House
Hampstead Road
London NW1 7QX

A BPCC plc Company

Pictures by Adrian Murrell/All-Sport

Frontispiece: Mike Gatting consults with his vice captain,
John Emburey, at the start of the tour

British Library Cataloguing in Publication Data

Gatting, Mike
    Triumph in Australia: Mike Gatting's 1986-87 cricket diary

    1. Test matches (Cricket)—Australia
    2. Test matches (Cricket)—England
    I. Title
    796.35'865   GV928.A8

    ISBN 0-356-14349-X

Typeset by York House Typographic
Printed and bound in Great Britain
by Butler & Tanner Ltd,
Frome and London

For my sons, Andrew and James, and my wife, Elaine, for her patience and understanding which allowed me to give my time to England.

Foreword by Micky Stewart

When Mike Gatting was invited to be captain of the 1986-87 side to Australia he was very much aware that the tour was going to be arguably the most important to England cricket in recent times. The results over the previous twelves months and the adverse press reports on and off the field had put the game into the doldrums and the whole image needed to be re-established. It was going to be a very hard job and Mike knew it.

After four and a half months of continuous cricket and travel Mike and his side had achieved what no one in their wildest dreams would have imagined – England had won the lot!

It was my privilege and pleasure to work closely with Mike in my role as Assistant Manager with responsibilities for the team's cricket and in my association with the first class game which goes back over thirty years I can't say I have enjoyed anything better than this particular tour.

I had also enjoyed the experience of playing with the late Ken Barrington for fifteen years and on many an occasion it has been said that when he walked to the wicket for England one could almost see the Union Jack draped round his shoulders. Mike Gatting projected this very same image both on and off the field and in the dressing room. He always sought to lead from the front no matter what the situation; an example being his willingness to bat at number three in the crucial first Test match at Brisbane when our early tour batting form had been riddled with inconsistencies and could not provide any kind of start to the innings. Another typical example was in the very last match of the tour, the second final of the World Series Cup at Sydney, when we were batting first and had amassed only a moderate total of 188 after a good start to the innings. There was apprehension in the dressing room with the players wondering if we were going to have to return to Melbourne to play a deciding match in the best of three finals. However, all the apprehension and depression disappeared after a few words from 'Gatt' which convinced everyone that 188 was more than enough on the Sydney pitch and the Australians wouldn't get anywhere near it. How right he was, but Neil Foster who had to bowl the last over will tell you that they got a lot nearer than he would have liked!

It wasn't only on the field that Mike showed a lot of courage. He was introduced to the demands of the international media in a most competitive country. Both English and Australian press expected him to show as much original skill at press conferences as he did tactically and with the bat out in the middle. Although he did not enjoy these moments during the first half of the tour it was typical of him that he battled it through so that public and press alike accepted him as he was and took him to their hearts.

Mike Gatting is a typical product of all that is good about English team games. He demands nothing less than he himself is prepared to give and always puts the side before himself. His uncomplicated bulldog determination sometimes hides a very intelligent cricketer with acute tactical awareness. In spite of the many years that have passed since my own playing days Mike and I have found that we have a lot in common in our outlook on the game and on the way that team games should be played.

Togetherness and harmony were the main ingredients of the England success in Australia. The policy was strongly spelt out before the trip began and the players responded excellently. No one would say that there wasn't the occasional hiccup, nor could it be said that the players were like angels. However, everyone made sure that the policy worked and all of them, led by Mike Gatting, could look each other in the eye and honestly say that they gave their all and it was very worth while.

Micky Stewart
May 1987

An ambition
fulfilled

At last I'd made it. Childhood dreams, hopes, aspirations had turned into reality. I was fulfilling the highest ambition of every English cricketer. Australia-bound for four months instead of being left behind for an English winter seeing out 1986 and bringing in 1987. Ahead lay the fight for the retention of the Ashes – still the series with a special magic and appeal of its own. The series in which the standing of the two sides in world rankings just doesn't matter.

I had always missed out when it had come around to Australia before, breeding a deep feeling of frustration and disappointment. My Test début was made in Pakistan back in 1977 when I was chosen ahead of Ian Botham. Tours to New Zealand, West Indies, India and Sri Lanka followed. Yet, whenever Australia loomed on the horizon, mine was the phone that never rang on the day they selected the tour party.

When my Middlesex captain Mike Brearley had finished finalising his squad for the 1978–79 and the 1979–80 tours, there was no room for me. The same applied when Bob Willis was in charge in 1982–83. I was beginning to think that I would never make it, my Australian cricketing experience limited to winters playing for local grade sides. Now I was off. Not just as a middle-order batsman, but as England's captain – with grateful thanks to David Gower. He was the man who gave me the chance, for backing me in 1984 when others had appeared to have lost their faith in my ability to serve my country, and giving me the right words of encouragment when I needed them most. I really did not think I had a chance of making the England side again for some while after I had been called in by David and the England selectors to try and stop the relentless march by the West Indies that summer towards their famous 'blackwash'. I was no more successful than the other batsmen, worse than some and out of the series before the summer was over. With my record, at that stage, I thought that would be it for another year at least.

Certainly the tour to India that winter looked a long way out of my reach. That was when David took a hand. Not only did he insist that I should be given another opportunity as a member of his touring side but also asked that I should go to India as his deputy. It was just the fillip my career needed at that stage.

David's action then was followed by even more encouragement when we arrived in India six weeks later. As the first Test in Bombay was about to start, we were all in need of comforting words. Just 48 hours earlier Percy Norris, the

Deputy British High Commissioner in Bombay, had been gunned down on his way to work only hours after he had entertained all of us so wonderfully at his home. We were not really in the right frame of mind to tackle India when we approached the First Test but David perked me up, strengthening my own resolve when he told me: 'Remember this time you are not on trial with perhaps a couple of Test matches to prove yourself. You're here as my vice captain which means that you are going to have to play all the way through. Make it work.' Having already allowed me to select the number three batting position in the Test side – the first time I had ever had a settled batting role for England during my eight-year career covering 30 Tests – I felt more relaxed than I had ever done playing for my country. More than that, I felt that I belonged. I celebrated my 'arrival' with my first Test century four days later.

Those memories jumped to the forefront of my mind as I made my way to the Westmoreland Hotel, just down the road from Lord's, on September 8 to occupy the chair David had filled just two years previously. The hotel is the usual place for selection meetings in London, especially when a touring side is involved. It is a place where dreams have been shattered for more than one player, although in destroying one dream the selectors have generally provided the opportunity for another player to take the first step along the road to possible stardom.

I was reminded of a story some years back when Surrey's opening bowler Robin Jackman was selected in the England 12 for a Test match at Lord's and arrived at the Westmoreland Hotel to book in on the the Wednesday lunchtime before the usual pre-Test practice session. He was convinced he had a good chance of making the final 11, resulting in a six-night stay at the hotel and was completely taken aback when the receptionist looked up the details of his room booking and announced: 'Ah, Mr Jackman, I've found your reservation. You're booked in for just two nights.' Sure enough, Jackers was made 12th man the following morning.

David had made me as a Test player when he had sat in the chair I was about to occupy, and I was acutely aware of the fact that I was going to play a leading role that evening in taking a decision that might end the Test career of one – if not more – of the players who had served under me in the series against India and New Zealand that summer. That was one part of a captain's role I did not fancy. But I had already discovered that skippering England was no easy task. In fact it had proved a painful lesson.

Even taking over the captaincy following the five-wicket defeat by India at Lord's after the first Test of the summer, had been a difficult and moving experience. I was very happy being David's second-in-command. I thought we had worked well together especially through India in 1984–85 and the following summer when the Australians had been routed. My deepest regret had been the delivery from Malcolm Marshall in the first one-day international against West Indies in Jamaica the previous February which had resulted in my nose having to be remodelled back in London. Regret, not because it hurt, but because it took me away from the West Indies at a vital stage of the Caribbean tour, just as the

First Test was being played. I'm not sure whether my presence as a batsman would have changed the course of the series or prevented us suffering another 'blackwash' but I had been in good form with the bat at the time and I like to think I could have been a considerable help to David both on and off the field, sharing his considerable load.

I was not expecting the change in leadership either. There had been some speculation in the newspapers, especially when David was re-appointed only for the first two one-day internationals and First Test. In fact, I don't think that any of us who had spent the previous two years working with David expected him to go. It was still quite a shock when Peter May, chairman of selectors, called me into the physiotherapist's room within minutes of the First Test match finishing and asked me if I was prepared to take over.

My first reaction was to ask for time to think things over, but he wanted an immediate response. I agreed to accept the responsibility and I doubt whether I would have reached any other decision even if I had been given a chance to sleep on it for a night. I'd never thought seriously about leading England, in the way that Allan Border had never seriously entertained the prospect of the Australian captaincy when he was asked to fill the role. But when such an offer is made, it is an honour you can't turn down.

David was marvellous about it all when I returned to the England dressing room that evening. He had learned of his sacking by then but there was no hint of embarrassment. He immediately handed over his 'I'm in charge' T-shirt which had been presented to him a week earlier when the selectors had suggested publicly that he should be a little more demonstrative in the field as a captain. The switch, however, was the start of a low period for me.

The atmosphere in the dressing room had not been right throughout that opening Test match against India. There was an air of unease and suspicion about the place. It was certainly not conducive towards playing our best cricket. Much of it was to do with the hangover effect from the pounding we had taken in the West Indies. I don't think anybody can appreciate just how drained we all felt by the time we left the Caribbean and the tension that accompanied us throughout those three months resulting from the unhealthy political side-issues. There had been less than a week between our return and plunging straight into another domestic season.

David's step-by-step re-appointment also had an unsettling affect and I was determined to put that right. I made it my first priority but it was not until five Test matches later, when we played New Zealand at the Oval in the final game, that I was happy with what I had achieved.

My start as a captain was none too impressive, losing to India at Headingley, when we were bowled out for 102 and 128, losing by 279 runs, and presenting India with the series although there was still one game of the three-match series remaining. We drew the Third Test against them, held New Zealand in the first match of the second series at Lord's but lost the second at Trent Bridge. It was during that match that I began to feel the strain of leadership for the first time.

By then I was coming under attack from the critics for both my tactical awareness and my form as a batsman. With two defeats in my first four Tests as captain, I suppose it was inevitable that some people would start to find fault with me tactically, but I was surprised by the suggestion I was finding it all too much and it was affecting my batting as well. I was amazed how people conveniently overlooked the fact that I had scored an unbeaten 183 at Edgbaston against India – an innings that started when we had lost Graham Gooch and Bill Athey without a run on the board – to help draw the Third Test.

I had taken that performance as a sign that I could handle both jobs, yet, by Trent Bridge, I found myself seeking out David Gower and asking his advice on how I should deal with the whole situation. He had gone through similar criticism in every series in which he led England – although he had often silenced the doubts by finishing top of the averages! He again offered words of comfort and told me I should never take the harsh words of uninformed critics to heart. Easy to say, not so easy to carry out.

It was too late for any of them to influence the selectors, because I had already been appointed for the Australian tour. So had the rest of the management team: Peter Lush, the Test and County Cricket Board's Promotions and Public Relations Executive was to have overall charge as manager, and be assisted by Micky Stewart, the former Surrey captain and England opener. We were also to have Laurie Brown with us again as the physiotherapist. He had built up a very good relationship with the team on his first tour of the West Indies and during the summer at home.

I was delighted with the combination. With Middlesex and the TCCB both being based at Lord's, I had got to know Peter quite well. He also travels to Test matches at home looking after the needs of the cricketing media and trying to smooth relations. At times they can become pretty strained, especially when we are losing. It results, quite naturally, in criticism which does make the players a little edgy although they will accept it from most as long as it does not become too personal. There are some writers, however, who go well over the top in this respect.

Where the relationship does become soured is when 'outsiders' are brought in. There are some newspapers who will not accept that England sometimes lose because they come up against a better side on the day. They start looking for other reasons to explain away defeats, rather than accept the word of their cricket writer that sides such as India and New Zealand are no longer the push-overs they were 20 years ago. This led to some outrageous scenes in the West Indies when newsmen and photographers hid in bushes outside the team hotel. With Peter's working knowledge of newspapers and the requirements of individual writers, he would be a tremendous asset in Australia, taking considerable weight off my shoulders.

The same applied to Micky. I did not know him particularly well but we had chatted about cricket many times when Middlesex visited the Oval where he was Surrey's cricket manager for a number of years, enjoying considerable success. I

Peter Lush, Tour Manager   *Micky Stewart, Assistant Manager*

liked his obvious enthusiasm for the game and discovered we thought along similar lines. This time Micky was being presented with even greater authority than any previous tour assistant manager. After discussions with Raman Subba Row, the chairman of the TCCB, it was agreed that Micky would be in complete charge of all practice sessions with the freedom to offer personal coaching to any individual if he felt they needed it. I was perfectly happy with the condition. Again it would take some of the pressure off as well as allowing me to concentrate on putting my own game in order rather than be occupied overseeing the nets.

Micky was not going to have a vote in the selection of the 16-strong tour party but he agreed to come up to Trent Bridge for the Second Test against New Zealand so that we could have a couple of days together and see if we were thinking along the same lines. By then I was already thinking of my own party, trying to narrow it down to around 20 names for discussion in September. I listened closely to the remarks of other players whenever individuals were discussed, went out of my way to talk to umpires, former players and cricket writers who had been touring with England for some years and knew the special problems involved. I thought we faced two areas of concern.

One of them was called Graham Gooch. The other was Ian Botham. By the time we reached Trent Bridge it had become clear that Graham was having serious doubts about making himself available for Australian selection. He was deeply affected by the visit to the West Indies where he was singled out for attack because of his past associations with South Africa, particularly the leadership of the so-called 'rebel' England side in 1982.

While others, such as John Emburey and Peter Willey, who had been in the side were able to shut their minds to the abuse of a few, Graham took it more personally. He was not satisfied with his form during the summer – he even suggested we might leave him out of the Test side on one occasion – and was concerned about being parted from his family for almost five months, his wife Brenda having given birth to twin girls two months earlier. He was asked to make a decision on his availability during the Trent Bridge Test but pleaded for extra time to think things over. I was naturally hoping he would agree to come but suspected then that his final answer would be 'no'.

Botham was a different concern. He was about to start playing first-class cricket again with Somerset after his period of suspension resulting from his admission in a newspaper article that he had smoked pot at some stage of his career. There was a large school of thought outside cricket's hierarchy – and some inside, I suspect – who believed Ian should not be selected whatever his form, claiming he would prove a disruptive influence.

Micky Stewart and I decided we would individually make contact with Ian to discuss his approach and attitude, even his willingness to tour under stricter disciplinary guidelines than on recent tours. We both came away from our separate conversations satisfied that he would give us each personally, and the team, 100 per cent support. That was good enough for me. I have had differences of opinion with Ian in the past but have never doubted his loyalty or his determination on the field to make England winners. What clinched it for me was the final Test against New Zealand at the Oval. Our poor record during the summer combined with Ian's tremendous hitting for Somerset in the three weeks he had been back playing first-class cricket, left the selectors and myself with no alternative but to recall him to the England side for that match. And if anybody still had reservations, they were swept away by the atmosphere in the dressing room when Ian reported for the normal pre-Test Wednesday practice session.

The change was remarkable. Just his presence in the side made all the others suddenly believe in themselves again. The dressing room had the right feel about it once more, the feel I had been trying to create all summer. We took the field the next day feeling confident for the first time that summer. When Ian took the wicket of Bruce Edgar with his first ball back in Test cricket to break New Zealand's opening partnership after the new-ball thrust had failed, there was talk of us winning again. It was a tragedy that the rain over the final two days denied us the chance of squaring that series.

By then Graham Gooch had made his decision to stay at home, leaving three main areas to resolve when I joined the other selectors, Peter May, Fred Titmus, Phil Sharpe and Alan Smith at the Westmoreland Hotel to select the tour party. We were joined by Peter Lush and Micky Stewart plus Raman Subba Row, Doug Insole, chairman of the TCCB's Overseas Tours Committee, Donald Carr, the secretary of the TCCB and Mike Gear, TCCB assistant secretary (cricket).

Looking at the heavy tour schedule and attempting to cover for every eventuality with the Test series plus the long list of one-day matches, I wanted to extend the party to 17. I felt this would have allowed me to take one extra quick bowler plus a young up-and-coming middle-order batsman. My request was turned down on the grounds that there would be insufficient cricket to keep everybody in form once the Test series started. It meant that Greg Thomas, the Glamorgan fast bowler, was to be the unlucky one on my list. Although he had not been a heavy wicket-taker during the summer and had not been at his best when called up for his one home Test appearance against New Zealand at Trent Bridge, I had seen enough evidence in the West Indies to suggest he would be more than useful in Australian conditions. His absence was heavily criticised in some newspapers when the tour party was announced, although nobody could suggest how we might have fitted him into the actual 16 named.

There was no question of leaving out any of the four pace bowlers we did select. Graham Dilley had proved a hard-working, number-one strike bowler during the summer, sadly missed when injured for two Test matches. It was impossible to argue against Neil Foster when he had taken 100 wickets in a summer for the first time to help Essex to the championship or the 97 taken by Phillip DeFreitas in proving the strong man of the Leicestershire attack. To complement these three we also needed Gladstone Small's ability to bowl a steady length and line at his sharp pace. Gladstone had one other fact in his favour. Earlier that year he had finished a season playing for South Australia in the Sheffield Shield competition with 37 wickets to his credit.

With Ian Botham to complete the pace bowling scene I was happy with the selection. I suppose 20-year-old DeFreitas surprised a number of people. He appeared to come from nowhere into the England reckoning in a short space of time. In fact I had been aware of him for a couple of years since he had played for Middlesex's second XI as a member of the Lord's groundstaff. When he started taking championship wickets I asked both David Gower and Peter Willey for an update and they both gave him a solid recommendation. They said he was genuinely quick when he needed to be in short bursts but could also do a good stock bowling job if necessary. That was good enough for me.

Most of the others picked themselves. Nobody could really argue with the main middle order of Gower, Allan Lamb and Botham. The one difficulty we had was in deciding between the two main claimants for the back-up position. Several were discussed but the issue boiled down to either Northants' Robert Bailey or Leicestershire's James Whitaker. I had admired them both at various stages during the summer. Their records were very similar, each showing steady improvement year after year which suggested they had digested the lessons and worked and overcome their weaknesses. It was felt, in the end, that Whitaker should be the one on the grounds that he was probably better off the back foot with the ability to play square either side of the wicket against the faster bowlers. He had certainly impressed me on that score facing up to Wayne Daniel in two lively Middlesex-Leicestershire encounters that summer.

There was nobody to challenge John Emburey for the off-spinning role, and although John Childs had enjoyed a staggering season with Essex to win admirers for his potential as the left-arm spinner, it was impossible to argue against the vast experience of Phil Edmonds. He was also the man in command and bowls particularly well in partnership with Emburey.

The wicket-keeping roles took up more time. It was difficult to decide one from the very talented bunch pressing for Bruce French's position in the England side, a group including Worcestershire's Steve Rhodes, who was an outstanding success on the England 'B' tour of Sri Lanka, Gloucestershire's nippy Jack Russell, David East of Essex and Surrey's Jack Richards. Paul Downton, who had lost his place to French during the summer, was also brought into the discussion with his record of stubbornness against fast bowling and calmness in one-day games. Richards won the final place largely on the grounds that he was the best one in form with the bat at the time of selection. On more than one occasion during the summer, he had saved Surrey in tense situations batting as high as number five. He is no slouch with the gloves either.

By far the most difficult decisions concerned the selection of the three opening batsmen. It occupied the most time before we agreed that Chris Broad, Bill Athey and Wilf Slack should be the right men for the task ahead.

Much was to be made later of the fact that Broad had not been selected once for England during the summer but was going on the tour, while we had left out Graeme Fowler, Tim Robinson, Martyn Moxon and Mark Benson who had all played Test cricket in 1986. Perhaps it did look a little strange, yet Broad had been mentioned at every Test selection meeting that I had attended over the summer. It was remarkable how often he had seemed to fail in a championship match just as we were picking a Test side. By the time the tour selection meeting had taken place, Broad had got his act together and was reeling off century after century.

With Athey having scored a classic hundred to help us win the second Texaco Trophy one-day international against New Zealand when opening the innings, we thought he deserved his place to act as cover opener or middle-order batsman. He is a superb technician who hadn't quite done himself justice by the end of the 1986 season, but we all felt that the real break for him was only just around the corner, one big innings and he could be a champion.

I suppose Slack was the most controversial choice when most newspaper critics had gone for a Robinson-Broad all-Nottinghamshire combination. Wilf had started the season badly but he was in tremendous form – like Broad – over the final month and I don't know any opener in England who looks so unperturbed when the ball is flying around head high. I argued his case.

These were tough decisions and I felt for others who just missed out. Apart from those I have already mentioned, Yorkshire opener Ashley Metcalfe and Kent's Richard Ellison – who destroyed Australia with his swing bowling towards the end of the 1985 series – could count themselves unlucky, but the team was picked in the knowledge that both would be playing in Australia during the winter and we could call upon them if necessary.

The only other question to be answered was the choice of vice-captain. There had been a call for David Gower to fill the role but I could understand the position of the selectors on that issue. Having dismissed David from the leadership only five Test matches earlier, they could hardly put him in a postion where he would end up captain again if anything happened to me. John Emburey was the only sensible choice. He is my deputy at Middlesex, a wise cricketer who shares my intense dislike of defeat. It was essential I should have somebody I could work closely with and I knew I would be able to do just that with John, even though we do not always agree on the best approach. There was one other important factor. The vice captain sits on the selection committee on tour and I thought John's voice was essential, offering a bowling viewpoint.

We all left that night satisfied with the choice and the balance of the party. I left particularly happy that it was a party that would also produce the vital dressing room atmosphere a winning team would need. I looked forward to seeing them all at Heathrow four weeks later. The final tour party consisted of the following players:

Mike Gatting	Middlesex (Captain)
John Emburey	Middlesex (Vice Captain)
Chris Broad	Nottinghamshire
Wilf Slack	Middlesex
Bill Athey	Gloucestershire
David Gower	Leicestershire
Allan Lamb	Northamptonshire
Ian Botham	Somerset
James Whitaker	Leicestershire
Bruce French	Nottinghamshire
Jack Richards	Surrey
Phil Edmonds	Middlesex
Graham Dilley	Kent
Neil Foster	Essex
Gladstone Small	Warwickshire
Phil DeFreitas	Leicestershire

Peter Lush (Manager)
Micky Stewart (Assistant Manager)
Laurie Brown (Physiotherapist)
Peter Austin (Scorer)

Settling in

Thursday 9 October

This is the moment. Lift-off day and Australia-bound as England's cricket captain. By the end of the day I can't help hoping the rest of the tour isn't going to be as chaotic. Most of the time the team room in the Skyways Hotel opposite Heathrow Airport had resembled a mad backroom scene at a fashion show with designers making final adjustments to gowns on models and being constantly forced to make quick changes. Our aim was to get the players looking smart for the 10.20pm departure – we nearly didn't make it!

With only a month between selection and departure, there had been no time for the lads to try out their team blazers and trousers until today. Almost everybody needed last-minute adjustments. When I tried on my own blazer I had a suspicion that if I did up the buttons at the front, the back seam would split open! Press conferences, television interviews, photocalls, all took place in between ironing boards, sewing machines and tailors lengthening or shortening sleeves, trouser legs and so on. They did a good job and by the time we held a small farewell party with TCCB officials, selectors and other friends, everybody had been sorted out – except for Ian Botham. Nothing the tailors did could make his gear fit and Ian was the only one not in uniform. Still, he always is different.

We had all reported the night before because Peter Lush, Micky Stewart and myself wanted to have a complete day with the players going through the tour details and giving them a chance to get to know each other better. I had a breakfast meeting with Peter and Micky. We called in the senior players just before lunch to get the views of Ian Botham, David Gower, Allan Lamb, John Emburey, Phil Edmonds and Graham Dilley who had all toured Australia before. It is important to get the build up to the First Test exactly right and I was keen to hear their views on how we should play it. It was a very informative meeting with Ian and Allan, both asking to play in every state match up to the First Test. I found their attitude very encouraging.

After lunch we had a team meeting where Peter went over the disciplinary demands and the reason why the code had been tightened in certain areas, particularly with regard to Press interviews.

There had already been two unfortunate incidents, starting with Ian being banned from appearing on an eve-of-tour Thames midweek sports programme. He complained bitterly when the ban was announced but the decision had been taken for the good of the whole party. We wanted to go there as a team and not a collection of individuals. Ian was even more upset when Phil Edmonds appeared on Terry Wogan's show along with his wife Frances without seeking permission. We were determined that similar incidents would not happen in Australia. Although Ian had been upset, the incident did have one advantage in showing the other players that the tour rules were not going to be bent for anybody. Ian accepted them completely when it was pointed out they were designed to protect rather than hinder him.

I was also to discover a little of the exposed, pressurised life Ian has to lead when we finally got through the customary checks at Heathrow and took the walk to the plane. There appeared to be photographers and television crews everywhere, each one pointed at Ian who was walking beside me. It was like being with a pop star as the flashbulbs went off in every direction with photographers crying 'this way Ian!' He took it all very well but I began to appreciate why he has snapped on occasions in the past.

Friday 10 October

The late departure of the previous night allowed us to drop off to sleep fairly quickly and I was pleased to see that even Ian had nodded off. He has so much energy that he often has trouble getting to sleep on flights. And if Ian is awake, he makes sure the others are around him, giving them a friendly – but powerful – tweak on the nose or ear at the slightest sign of dropping off. He slept for five hours on the first leg, four on the next and even managed another five hours on the final haul. It was heaven.

I took special notice of the younger players to make sure they were mixing in. I was very pleased to see that Phil DeFreitas and James Whitaker, the two very new boys from Leicestershire, already seemed at home in the party. On previous tours I had noticed that some 'new boys' had appeared a little overawed and had been left on one side, not sure how they should approach more senior and experienced players. Not so 'Daffy' and 'Jumbo', which said a lot for their confidence. I settled down for my second nap happy with the mix aboard. It had been something that had worried me after the events of the summer but the early signs were good.

The only note of concern on the trip was Allan Lamb spending part of his tour money on a compact disc stereo player at Singapore Airport and I guessed we were in for a noisy time now and again throughout the next four and a half months. Allan is another lively specimen always ready for a laugh. He spent much of the journey teasing Peter Lush about the column he said he was writing for his local weekly paper, saying he wasn't going to bother having it vetted – it was only a joke though!

Saturday 11 October

Arrival in Sydney at breakfast time and transfer to a domestic flight for the final leg of the journey to Brisbane which was to be our 'home' for the first fortnight. Another two hours of hanging around, clearing immigration and customs which is always a frustrating time. There was also my first confrontation with the Australian media, something I had not been looking forward to with any great enthusiasm. They all wanted to talk to Ian but our rules were clearly spelt out by Peter Lush and they had to be content with Peter, Micky and myself. The press conference turned out to be much better than I had expected.

I had prepared myself to face awkward, probing questions, expecting to be accused of leading the worst England team ever to visit Australia in the history of the game, an accusation that appears to have been thrown at every previous England captain upon arrival. I was ready with my answers in defence of the side but never had to use them. The press conference was an extremely friendly affair. Maybe it was because of the early hour of our arrival, coinciding with dawn. Or perhaps that several of the leading cricket writers were away in India covering Australia's short, three-Test tour. Anyway, I departed with a sense of relief.

The real killer was the delay and the final flight to Brisbane. It took just an hour but we felt we had already been up all day by the time we arrived at the Crest Hotel, and lunch was still an hour away. There was another frustrating delay when it was discovered that some rooms were not suitable. Sharing is the order of the day on tours and some of the lads had been given rooms containing only one bed plus a couch. With the hard work schedule we had planned, it was essential everybody should have a good bed to provide the best chance of sleeping off the fatigue and recovering ready for the next round. Eventually everybody was satisfied.

Although tired after the flight I was determined to stay awake as long as I could in an attempt to get over possible jet lag in one long sleep. I decided on nine holes of golf along with John Emburey, Graham Dilley, Chris Broad, James Whitaker and Gladstone Small. It was not as successful as it might have been. For a start our taxi driver dropped us at the wrong spot and we were left with a two-mile jog to the clubhouse. The first Aussie plot I wonder? The golf wasn't much better. There were a few lakes around the course and between us I think we managed to land a ball in every one we came across. Still, it proved a useful way of making sure we stayed awake until mid-evening. We were ready for bed around nine. All except Ian. He took himself off to watch the first of three finals for the Australian basketball championship between Brisbane Bullets and Adelaide 36ers. Another example of his remarkable reserves of energy.

Sunday 12 October
Managed a good night's sleep to prepare for our first training session at the Church of England School where the practice facilities were excellent. They looked after us very well. We suffered two early casualties. Peter Lush had woken up with a painful toe which was diagnosed as gout. He'll cop some stick from the lads during the rest of the tour. In the nets Neil Foster got his wrist in the way of an Ian Botham return drive. Nothing serious, fortunately.

Micky trained us hard. It was probably tougher than most expected for the first work-out just 24 hours after booking into our hotel, but everybody accepted his authority. He had taken great care over planning the opening sessions so that they never became boring and repetitive. Boring nets can do more harm than good if the players switch off and just go through the motions. Micky demonstrated his footballing background – he played professionally for Charlton following an amateur career with Corinthian Casuals during which he played in an Amateur Cup Final replay – with a four-a-side game to help make the players quicker over a few yards.

By the end I felt very tired. I had started the tour with a cold developing and it was beginning to come out this evening, forcing me to bed early. Most of the others took a similar decision. Jet lag was still with us.

Monday 13 October
I discovered today just how busy life can be for a touring captain, especially in Australia. It left me even more grateful that Peter and Micky were around to take some of the load off my shoulders. I had to get up early for a television interview for Channel Nine who have the TV cricket rights in Australia. They sell the game hard here and I can see that Peter is envious of the exposure the game gets, particularly the way it is pushed on the Channel Nine network. There is just nothing like it at home, which is a pity. Perhaps the BBC could do more.

My first television interview was at 7.45am for the breakfast show, and my phone is hardly ever quiet in my room. Phone calls start coming in from early morning onwards from various small radio stations all around Australia, each one wanting a snap interview. David Gower had warned me I would be inundated but I was still taken by surprise today. David has warned me, too, about the early morning interviewer who tries to catch you unawares. He'll wake you up, announce you are live on the air and start pumping questions before you are fully awake enough to appreciate what is happening. But so far so good. The interviewers have all been very friendly and it is heartening to see the interest the tour is creating.

That was followed by another long training session with all the bowlers operating for an hour at least. We returned for more in the afternoon. Micky is getting us into shape very quickly but limbs are beginning to ache. Bed still beckons at an early hour.

Tuesday 14 October
Another early rise, another breakfast time television interview, this time conducted in a nearby park to provide an outdoor background. I am now feeling very tired with the cold having spread to my chest making breathing difficult and Laurie Brown has issued a course of antibiotics. We had a full-scale practice session out in the middle under match conditions with some of the attending media lending a hand as fielders. They were sharper than I thought they might be! It proved very exhausting which was just what Micky wanted. 'They need to know what it feels like to be knackered after a day in the field under a hot sun so they will not be taken by surprise when it happens,' Micky told the media afterwards.

Despite the legs feeling heavy and the breathing difficult I agreed to join Ian, David and Allan for 18 holes of golf. By the time we arrived at the 18th the game was all square but it was so dark we could only just make out the flag. Following the ball was near impossible. My partner Allan Lamb stretched himself out on the ground behind me when I played my approach shot because it was the only way we could see whether I was playing the right line and judge where the ball would land. Surprisingly, the system worked and we beat David and Ian on the last hole. The members thought we were mad playing in the dark and gave us a little friendly Aussie stick when we reached the club house for much needed thirst-quenchers.

Tonight Micky, Peter and I chatted to some of the senior players about how things had worked out over the first three days. There was a suggestion that we had pushed them a little hard at the start and we decided to give everybody the following day off as a reward for their efforts. That decision was quickly changed when we discovered that rain was forecast for Thursday which would have meant two days without practice. Thursday became the rest day instead.

Wednesday 15 October

I became the first serious tour casualty today. My chest was so painful and with my throat swollen, there was no way I could get out of bed for the practice which Micky had arranged at the Gabba Test ground where we were to take on Queensland in the opening first-class match of the tour on Friday week and Australia in the First Test on November 14. He wanted to give all the new players a taste of the ground and a feel of the background when it came to taking catches. I did manage to get up in the evening to attend the first official function of the tour given on behalf of the Lord Mayor of Brisbane (although the Lord Mayor wasn't there – he was actually in Lausanne helping to present Brisbane's case for staging the 1992 Olympic Games).

On return to the hotel I was a little perturbed to find one English newspaper had carried a story about senior players complaining the practice sessions had been too tough under a large back-page headline 'England Players in Revolt'. The *Sun* was the culprit and it was disappointing after the efforts we had made to accommodate all the wishes of the media from the first moment we had got together. They quoted a player without naming him which always arouses my suspicions about the accuracy of the quote or the story. All the senior players I spoke to were equally concerned for they had appreciated the way we had consulted them over the practice sessions. They had been pushed hard but admitted they felt better for it. I had been extremely pleased the way the net sessions had gone, particularly encouraged by the attitude of the players. The *Sun* story was false and misleading, something we could have done without. . .

The net sessions had produced one great bonus too. Ian Botham was swinging the ball again, and swinging it both ways. He looked more like the Ian of three years ago as far as his bowling was concerned and all the batsmen were coming out of the nets talking enthusiastically about him.

Thursday 16 October

The lads had their rest day but it proved a busy one for me. This morning there were more radio interviews as our first match approached against a Queensland Country XI over three days at Bundaberg. It was followed by our first selection committee meeting of the tour, a two-hour indoor net session against a bowling machine to make up for missing yesterday's practice and then the first social committee meeting.

The selection committee meeting proved quite straightforward in the end with the 12 for Bundaberg virtually picking themselves. We obviously had to start by giving our opening pair of Chris Broad and Wilf Slack a match together to help them adjust to the style of each other. We also needed Bill Athey in the team as the cover opening batsman. Although he does not open for Gloucestershire, we had not ruled him out of contention for one of the opening roles in the Test series. We felt it essential that all three should be given an early opportunity to fight for the two places available. There was no problem fitting Bill in because Allan Lamb was still not match fit following a minor knee operation at home shortly before we set off for Australia.

That produced a batting order of Broad, Slack, Athey, Gower, Gatting and Botham. Bruce French was the wicket-keeper in possession and we decided it was only right that he should have first crack at keeping his Test place and we decided to use both spin bowlers. The one difficulty was deciding on the pace attack. We wanted to see Graham Dilley stretch himself under match conditions and we finally opted for Phil DeFreitas who had been the most impressive of the faster bowlers in the nets and certainly the quickest. The young lad who was born in Dominica was creating considerable interest among the Australian media and I was pleased to see the level-headed way he was coping with all the attention. It was an indication he would not be overwhelmed if he should make the Test side at the age of 20. When announcing the team I had to admit that it had a Test look about it, apart from finding room for a fit Allan Lamb, but I was quick to stress we were still leaving all our options open.

The social committee was in good form. David Gower had been made chairman, Lamb the treasurer responsible for the collection of fines, with Graham Dilley the secretary. They are good, fun sessions essential to any tour party, especially if the going gets a little rough – and the fines were soon being handed out! John Emburey was the first victim, fined for leaving Graham Gooch behind. They are the greatest of pals who are seldom apart on tour – indeed Ian Botham called them Hansel and Gretel some tours ago! In the end it was decided to reduce the amount of the fine on the grounds that John had also been away from Graham too long. It was a good note on which to end the day, with the first of our 32 internal flights around Australia scheduled for early the next morning.

Friday 17 October

The energy of Micky Stewart never ceases to amaze me. Throughout the first week of practice he had been the first one on the field, the last to finish, willing to spend extra time coaching individual players in addition to organising the nets and the fielding. Today he seemed to pop up everywhere. He decided that we should go straight to the cricket ground for practice after our arrival in Bundaberg before getting to our motel on the Queensland coast where the Pacific ocean laps the sandy beach outside our room windows.

Micky organised the fielding practice after Laurie Brown had taken us through our warm-up exercises. Then he kept one eye on the nets more than 100 yards away whilst overseeing Ian bowling off his full run out in the middle helped by Steve Rhodes, the Worcestershire wicketkeeper who was playing in the local cricket league for the winter. He had turned up to give us a hand. Micky was everywhere, demanding but ever cheerful. Once again I was able to appreciate his support especially as I was still far from being 100 per cent fit. The first lot of antibiotics had not worked and I was now on a second course but the chest was still painful. I would have missed the game if it had not been the opening match.

Bundaberg itself was a pleasant enough place to launch the tour. Wide streets decorated by gaily coloured tropical bushes which were matched by the bright plumage of the parakeets screeching in the trees overhead. It is a sugar town famous for its rum – a Bundy and dry being a popular drink in Australia.

With the practice taking up a couple of hours, we didn't have time to sample the beach for any length of time. No sooner had we completed the 30-minute drive to book in at our hotel, than we were driving back again for an official welcome at the ground which caused great amusement. The official speech became a 30-minute act from a lively local character giving views of a young Australian couple who had just watched the Romeo and Juliet balcony scene. He read his lines with great passion and feeling which caused Allan Lamb to double up with laughter, shouting 'more'. David Gower was also doubled up on the coach ride back, but that was for a different reason!

We did not stay as long as perhaps some of the local people wanted but the day had started early. We needed to get to our beds. There was a great relief that the cricket was starting, the practice sessions at an end. We had come to play cricket and were keen to find out exactly what shape we were in.

Teething troubles

Saturday 18 October

The tour was officially launched today about 10 minutes after the start of the game. That was when I heard the first Aussie shout of 'ave a go, you mugs!' That was a bit unfair considering the way Wilf and Chris had been hitting the ball around from the opening overs but I suppose no cricket match in Australia is complete without that call. The Queensland Country XI bowling wasn't the greatest in the world and the wicket was just right for batting but I was pleased with the first day's performance. Whatever the standard of the bowling, the runs still have to be made and only David Gower missed out on the opportunity to spend some time at the crease. He was there for less than three overs before being stumped and I would have liked him to have been around a little longer in re-introducing himself to Australian conditions. His dismissal did contain a message for the others. Whatever the standard of the bowling, and David had watched the openers put on 160 for the first wicket, it is still necessary to have a look at the opposition and the conditions before striking out.

The most encouraging aspect of the day was Wilf making runs. He had looked a little out of touch during the practice week in Brisbane, not moving his feet as well as we would have liked and showing a tendency to push at the ball rather than go through with his strokes. Chris confirmed his net form, while Bill was sheer perfection, an ideal model for any youngster to watch. The crowd were given value for money when Ian scored his half century in the last 20 minutes. I'd also enjoyed myself, hitting the first century of the tour which left me wondering whether the game might be first-class, although I suspected it was not, with the opposition not having one player in their side with state experience. Manager Peter Lush confessed he wasn't sure.

Sunday 19 October

It was confirmed today by the Press that the match was not first-class. It was disappointing. It meant that I'd have to wait for my first first-class century in Australia. More disappointing was the fact that the town of Bundaberg had copped the centre of a tropical electric storm the previous evening, although it had been relatively dry where we were on the coast. By dawn the outfield had been under water. Despite the great efforts of the groundstaff, the start was delayed which messed up my first intention which was to bat on and attempt to win by an innings.

Instead I was forced to declare in the hope that we would be able to bowl the Country XI out by the end of the day. We failed to do that but what play there was helped to confirm my initial impression that Daffy DeFreitas would play a key role in this tour. He was the sharpest of the bowlers and the key figure in a run out, with a return from the boundary edge right over the stumps that owed a lot to his Caribbean upbringing. It was a magnificent flat throw following a pick-up on the run, taking the batsman completely by surprise.

Monday 20 October

More disappointment today. Another overnight storm left the outfield in a mess and it was not really fit to play even when we started after lunch. We agreed to carry on because we felt we owed the local association a duty to have a go for all the effort they had put into the match. They had looked after us well.

The delay ruined my plans for the match even though we dismissed the rest of the Country XI batsmen quickly with Daffy snapping up three quick wickets, as a fast bowler should do when up against rabbits. I decided against enforcing the follow on in a victory attempt – I had announced to the media it would be my intention to go for a win in every game, although in the interests of the tour as a whole I thought it would be better to give our batsmen who had not got to the wicket during the first innings a chance to get a feel of what it was like at the crease in match conditions. Bruce French took full advantage in opening the second innings, spending the three hours remaining at the crease for a half century.

We did suffer one setback when a few of us decided to get some exercise during the morning hold-up by playing football, the nets having been ruined by the rain. We found a large area of open grass, but the game had to be called off when Bill Athey finished up with a calf-muscle injury which left him limping badly. I was responsible, although it had been completely accidental, catching Bill on the calf as we went up for a high ball. It was a typical football injury leaving Bill with what is known as a 'dead leg' in that profession. It was nothing serious but bad enough to put Bill out of the next match. I made a mental note to go easy on the use of the football before a Test match. We could not risk that sort of thing happening again.

England XI v Queensland Country XI
Played at Bundaberg, Oct 18, 19, 20

England XI 491 for 4 dec (M.W. Gatting 171, B.C. Broad 97, C.W.J. Athey 73*
W.N. Slack 70, I.T. Botham 52*) and 129 for 3 (B.N. French 63*)
Queensland Country XI 160 (L. Shulte 78* A.J. DeFreitas 4 for 37)

Match Drawn.

Tuesday 21 October

Had a meeting with Micky this morning to discuss the lessons learned during the first match and decided there was no need to change any of our original ideas regarding the lead in to the Test series.

There was some outside concern about the number of no-balls Graham Dilley had delivered in Bundaberg and Micky decided to have a close look at him during the nets at the Gabba. Ian Botham also had a talk with 'Picca' offering him hints on how to make sure he got his approach perfectly right. That was nice to see. Picca was not particularly concerned, however, saying he expected to bowl a few right at the start of the tour when he stretched himself for the first time. He was confident it would not be a problem. We decided not to make a big issue of it because we did not want Graham to reach the stage where he would be concentrating so much on the bowling crease at his end, he would not be thinking of the batsman at the other. That would not do him or us any good. Our softly, softly approach was settled when DeFreitas, who had been fielding at mid-off, said the umpire concerned had over-reacted and that some of the no-balls called had been perfectly fair deliveries.

Wednesday 22 October

Ian Botham made me an offer last night which I felt I could not refuse. That was the opportunity to go deep-sea fishing today although it meant getting up at 3.45am while the rest of the lads had a few more hours in bed before setting off for Lawes to play a one-day match against another Queensland Country XI. With Allan Lamb having decided he was now match fit, although still wearing a brace to give his knee support, and the need to play James Whitaker for the first time, I decided to miss the match anyway. There would not be many opportunities to take a match off on the tour.

It was a marvellous experience even though I finished up feeling a little sea-sick and wobbly when the seas started cutting up rough. Needless to say, Ian caught the big one and I missed out, the typical fisherman's story of the one that got away. The sea was calm and the weather ideal when we set out in a well-equipped yacht that had been arranged for us by Jeff Thomson. It was good to get away and relax without cricket dominating my thoughts and the day was made for me when a school of dolphins swam around the yacht, leaping out of the water – a fascinating sight. Early on we had a small marlin on one of the lines but it didn't take the hook properly and got away.

We spent some time looking for more strikes and got two bites simultaneously. Ian took the first and was strapped for the battle ahead, I moved in for the second line and found myself engaged in a fight to land what was obviously a fairly large fish. It was quite a strain on the arms and shoulders, playing the fish for more than half an hour. Letting it run, then winding it in a little before the fish made another strike to get away. Both Ian and I were winning when, unfortunately, the lines became entangled as the fish made another attempt to escape. My line snapped leaving Ian to land a handsome 70lb sailfish at the end of his hour-long fight. Ian immediately arranged to have the fish treated and shipped home so that it could take pride of place in his big-game trophy cupboard that has many spectacular scalps.

Although I was very tired by the time we returned to the hotel, I waited for Micky and John Emburey to report on the success of the day. They told me Allan Lamb had started his tour in tremendous fashion with a century. His knee had come through the examination despite one slight twinge early on when he was forced to turn sharply and regain his ground. He was going to be fit for the opening match of the first-class programme.

The openers had put down another nice platform which was very promising and the only disappointment had been Whitaker getting out for a duck on his first England opportunity. The Country XI batsmen had resisted better than in the first game but had been so tied down by accurate bowling, they never threatened to match our total. Daffy had again proved the pick of the bowlers.

England XI v S.E. Queensland Country XI
Played at Lawes, Oct 22

England XI 245 for 9 (50 overs) (A.J. Lamb 111)
S.E. Queensland Country XI 187 for 6 (50 overs)

England XI won by 58 runs.

Thursday 23 October

Met up with Allan Border today and the other Queensland players, Greg Ritchie and Craig McDermott, who had been on Australia's tour of India where they had tied the First Test and batted stubbornly on the last day of the third to draw the series. They had returned home two days earlier and they all looked remarkably fit when they arrived at the Gabba ground to attend a lunch to mark the start of Queensland's cricket season. There is nothing like a tour of India or Pakistan to trim people into shape. All three had suffered stomach problems I gathered.

We had all followed the progress of the final Test match in Bombay with great interest especially on the final day when Australia looked likely to lose. They managed to bat through that last day losing only three wickets to avoid defeat and Allan appeared a much happier and relaxed man than the last time I had met up with him as Australia's captain. Twice in the previous eight months he had talked openly of giving up the captaincy, but spending two-thirds of the summer in the relaxing company of the Essex players had obviously done him good.

At the selection committee meeting today we decided to go into the game against Queensland with what looked like being our Test line-up. Chris and Wilf had given us two good starts in the country matches and deserved the first crack at establishing themselves as the opening pair against a state attack although we had not ruled Bill Athey completely out of contention as an opener. He could have played against Queensland at a pinch but although he was much better there was no point in risking his calf injury at such an early stage of the tour.

For the same reason we decided at the last minute not to risk Graham Dilley who had been complaining of a sore ankle. He has to have it heavily strapped before every game and there was no point in him risking extra damage. Even without him we still entered the game with a strong-looking side. I was confident we would do well in this opening encounter.

Had dinner this evening with Micky and a few of the lads, going out of the hotel for once. It resulted in Micky gaining a new nickname. We opted for a Chinese restaurant, much to his disgust. 'Can't stand the stuff,' he said. 'when I have a meal I want to feel fed and content.' We persuaded him to come along and, for somebody who doesn't like Chinese food, it was remarkable how often the revolving centrepiece of the table stopped in front of him so that he could take another helping. He was christened 'China' on the spot.

Friday 24 October
Calamity, I suppose, would be about the right word to describe it. After the big build up, the big let-down. All out for 135 and nobody to blame but ourselves. I'd lost the toss and Border sent us in on a well-grassed wicket but that was not the reason for our downfall. I made a mental note that despite the grass, the ball did nothing startling and the wicket was a little on the slow side.

The slowness of the wicket played a part in our collapse, coupled with the tension in the dressing room with the players all feeling in good nick and eager to get on with the scoring. Unfortunately we proved too keen. Apart from Wilf, we all fell to attacking strokes, getting out before we had really tasted the pitch or paid as much attention as we should have done to the left arm slant of Harry Frei and Dirk Tazelaar, the two bowlers who did the bulk of the damage.

They were supported by some good catching, particularly by Robbie Kerr in the gully – I was one of his victims – and although I was disappointed over the size of our effort, I wasn't deeply concerned with it being the first day of the important games. I just hoped that everybody would have learned a lesson from our collapse and, if taken to heart, we would benefit and build on it. Micky had a quiet word, stressing the importance of being patient and being more selective in which deliveries to leave entirely alone.

Saturday 25 October
The Australian media made a great play about our first-day demise and I couldn't help wondering over breakfast what our own English travelling corps had made of yesterday's proceedings. If it had been in the same language, it would have made depressing reading over the breakfast tables back home. Unfortunately we made things even worse for ourselves during the first period today when we allowed Queensland openers Kerr and Andrew Courtice to escape during an opening 154-run partnership. It should never have got beyond 50.

Most worrying was the sight of Bruce French missing a relatively easy catch behind as well as a stumping. It was extraordinary for someone who had kept so well at home last summer when given his Test cap at my first selection meeting. I can recall now at least three magnificent catches, particularly one down the leg side few other wicketkeepers would have reached, let alone held.

I felt much better about our position at the end of the day. All the pace bowlers had performed well with Daffy getting a little more life out of the wicket than Craig McDermott had done on the first day. Gladstone Small also bowled a good line in picking up three wickets. With our catching also improving after lunch, we clawed our way back well as Queensland slipped from 154 without loss to 311 for seven before Border declared. That gave him the chance to slip us in again for four overs which proved disastrous for Wilf who was out for a duck during a fine over from Frei which must have suprised even him. Still, I went to bed a little happier.

Sunday 26 October

We were saved from an unexpected quarter today after another disappointing start that had begun to worry me. Neil Foster was the hero, making sure that there was no chance of us being defeated inside three days as had seemed possible at one stage. He hit a career-best, undefeated 74 coming in at number ten which even gave us an outside chance by the end of the day of bringing off a surprise win. 'Fozzy' fancies himself a little with the bat and is a good, clean striker when playing straight. He came off the field muttering 'Tell Both to watch out, I'm after his all-rounder role!'

My concern was over the top of the order. Having lost Wilf on the second evening, we slumped to 99 for five, which at least was a little better than our first innings. This time I was one of the batsmen to fail when I played back instead of forward to Brett Henschell, a gentle off spinner who bowled Bob Willis' side to defeat in the opening match here four years earlier. Getting out like that, I couldn't really say much to the others.

Ian Botham was having no nonsense. With Allan Lamb giving him solid support, despite being hit painfully on the foot which forced him to ask for a runner, Ian took Queensland apart. He littered the ground with boundaries, one straight six clearing the boundary and the dog track which surrounds the playing area and smashing a window in the Queensland Cricket Association office. They put on 122 together for the sixth wicket in 83 minutes, but we were still only just over 50 ahead when Fozzy came in at the fall of the eighth wicket and took over where Ian had left off. The last two wickets added 108 in 86 minutes under Fozzy's onslaught, until he ran out of partners.

McDermott came in for some stick from Fozzy, too. The young Australian fast bowler, fighting for his Test place after failing to take wickets in India, became flustered under the attack and Gladstone Small was once forced to duck hurriedly under a beamer.

We in cricket all like to believe that these deliveries – a head-high full toss –

are accidental, a product of nerves or sweaty palms but Craig produced more than one in England when the Australians were taking a hammering in 1985. The one today provoked harsh words from Allan Border who appeared more upset to see it than Gladstone. He immediately whipped McDermott out of the attack. The relationship between the two sides in 1985 was very good and Allan was obviously making sure the same would happen on this tour. I was more than willing to co-operate.

Monday 27 October

Nothing could save us going down to our first defeat. With Queensland starting the day needing just another 106 with eight wickets left and the pitch playing easily, I had expected it. My one hope was a storm promised for just after lunch but Greg Ritchie and Border proved equal to my attempts to slow the game down. Border hit the winning run in the last over before lunch, the rain came down about an hour later.

Our five-wicket defeat excited the press corps of both camps with the Australian writers insisting our morale must be low, attitude wrong and batting hopeless, whatever I said to the contrary during the after-match interviews all captains have to suffer. I say 'suffer' because my England captaincy experience to date had always found me on the back foot on these occasions. The most sensible words came from Allan Border who said Queensland's win would obviously give Australia a psychological boost, but he wasn't reading too much into it.

I knew the papers would not make pleasant reading in the morning but some of the heat was taken out of our situation by a story in the *Sun* newspaper at home saying Ian Botham had signed to play for Queensland during the next three English winters and he would never tour again. The other papers had mentioned that Ian was thinking of playing for Queensland but the *Sun* had gone over the top again, much to Ian's displeasure. Ian immediately became the target of numerous media enquiries, a situation that demonstrated the wisdom of having Peter Lush as manager. With his experience of coping with the media, he was able to shield Ian whilst arranging a press conference to clear up the situation immediately the match finished.

I was quite pleased to hear Ian had confirmed on the record that this would be

---

England XI v Queensland
Played at Brisbane, Oct 24, 25, 26, 27

England XI 135 and 339 (I.T. Botham 86, N.A. Foster 74* A.J. Lamb 65)
Queensland 311 for 7 dec (R.B. Kerr 95, A.B. Courrice 70)
and 164 for 5 (G.M. Ritchie 52)

Queensland won by 5 wickets.

---

his last England tour. Not because I did not want him around in the future – England will miss him desperately overseas – but because it meant that he would be keen to go out in a blaze of glory, and that can only be good for the rest of us in the Ashes' series.

Tuesday 28 October

Today was not a day I wish to have repeated on this tour, although I suspect there will be more like it to come as we criss-cross Australia on a schedule that may suit Australian cricket domestically but does nothing for us. Somebody has counted we will be making 32 internal flights alone. With the number of times we put down at other airports en route, that will mean somewhere around 100 take-offs and landings before we are through. Not a pleasant thought for anybody who doesn't like flying. Graham Dilley is our worst passenger and after today Peter Lush, Bill Athey and myself are also not too keen to get in another plane.

We had an early start to get from Brisbane to Wuddina (pronounced Woodna), to play a one-day game against South Australia Country XI tomorrow. The route was via Sydney and Adelaide, changing planes each time and finishing up on a 50-seater Belfast-built Short Brothers aircraft for the final leg to Wuddina. It is a comfortable enough plane – unless you hit rough weather. We did.

I was so engrossed in taking even more money off John Thicknesse of the *London Standard* during the hour-long flight from Adelaide I did not notice the early rough passage as I concentrated on my cards. The worst was still to come, hitting a particularly violent patch of weather just as we landed. By this time I had put the cards away and needed both hands to grip the seat as we were tossed around all over the place. The queasy feeling that began to build up in my stomach was not helped by the pilot banking sharply in doing a circle of the airport before landing instead of going straight in. Peter Lush, sitting up front alongside Wilf Slack, was the first to reach for the sickbag much to Allan Lamb's merriment at the back. Picca Dilley went decidedly white, my stomach was lurching by the time the plane touched down and Bill Athey's legs became so wobbly, he collapsed on the tarmac as soon as his feet hit the ground.

The local welcoming committee couldn't have been too impressed by our state on arrival. It took a few minutes for us all to pull ourselves together. The local people began to have more respect for us later when Allan and Phil Edmonds took some of them on at darts and bowls when we reached our 'pub' – and beat them.

The local association had been inundated with ticket applications to attend a dinner they had arranged for us tonight at the cricket ground, some people travelling more than 200 miles to see us. They did their best to accommodate everybody but it put a strain on the kitchen staff. By the time our coach arrived three hours later to pick us up for our return journey, poor Neil Foster had not even started his main course. He was determined to stay for his meal despite our attempts to get him to leave – he eats well for somebody of his lean build. I was all right because I had made sure I was one of the first in. The lads said that was nothing unusual.

Wednesday 29 October

Our thoughts today were mainly concentrated on the return air trip to Adelaide in the same plane that had brought us to Wuddina. We still managed to do enough on the field however to win the match comfortably on a magnificent batting wicket that was a tribute to the town.

It is one of the rare grass wickets in this area, a group of local volunteers having the foresight some 20 years earlier to switch from concrete and matting, although it meant digging up and transporting suitable soil from some foothills 20 or so miles away. They each deserved a medal for their splendid work. Despite the quality of the wicket, the Country XI batsmen could do little against our bowling and were restricted to 131 for nine off their 50 overs. Chris Broad and Wilf Slack helped themselves to half centuries each in knocking off the runs. It was pleasing to see Wilf looking a little more like the batsman I know at Middlesex and he was taking no chance in having his mood spoilt on the flight back to Adelaide. He refused to sit next to Peter Lush this time, Fozzy being awarded that privilege. Fortunately the flight was a beauty and no sick bags were needed.

England XI v S. Australia Country XI
Played at Wudinna, Oct 29

S. Australia XI 131 for 9 (50 overs) (J. Mitchell 68)
England XI 135 for one (B.C. Broad 59, W.N. Slack 54*)

England XI won by 9 wickets.

Thursday 30 October

With the First Test now only a fortnight away, one or two problem areas had started to appear and the selection panel had a long meeting last night in an attempt to solve them whilst still giving everybody a chance to compete for places.

Wilf and Chris had opened so far but we decided to team up Chris with Bill Athey for the four-day state game against South Australia starting tomorrow. Wilf was still not completely happy with his form and rather than risk another low score which might set him back further, we decided he would be better off having net sessions under Micky for four days in an attempt to solve his technical problems.

David Gower was also a puzzle. We needed him to spend some time in the middle to find his touch and the Adelaide Oval surface is generally regarded as the best one in Australia. We were very tempted to play him although he finds it difficult to motivate himself for these warm-up matches. In the end we decided he would be better having the match off because he would certainly play in the final state game against Western Australia before the First Test. The need to play a long innings then, we felt, would help his concentration. I wasn't too worried about his lack of runs. He had looked good in the nets, a touch player who needs only to stroke one magnificent boundary off the middle of the bat to transform him from an ordinary batsman into being the best left-hander in the world. Leaving him out was more a protective move to shield him from himself. He gets tired and, to a certain extent, irritable when questioned about his form every time he fails to make at least 50 at the wicket.

Leaving him out also gave us the opportunity to bring in his Leicestershire colleague James Whitaker for his first first-class innings. I was very keen to see him at the crease. He is a very ambitious young man who dreams of playing for England for the next ten years. No doubt playing alongside David has helped fire that dream and he looks to have the ability to carry it off.

The clouds thicken

Friday 31 October

The Adelaide Oval is the most English of the Australian grounds. There are no huge floodlight pylons to dominate the scene; one side of the ground is completely open, affording a lovely view of the trees in the adjoining park with the Adelaide Hills rising beyond. The pitch looked the beauty I expected it to be, which suited me. I knew the faster bowlers would get little out of it and this gave me the chance to use John Emburey and Phil Edmonds for a long spell when David Hookes decided to bat first. I felt they needed a hard work-out.

I was proved right when they first came on to bowl, neither particularly impressive in their opening overs, having difficulty finding the right line. Phil was the more wayward at the start, giving too many runs away through the off-side when we had agreed on a six-three leg-side field in order to keep the batsmen in check, the boundary either side of the wicket being very short.

By the end of today they – and I – were much happier. The pair had established a firm control and only the very best of the South Australian batsmen were able to cope. Wayne Phillips, who has given up wicket-keeping since touring England in 1985, scored a century. Glen Bishop, who partnered him in a 144 third-wicket stand, looked even more impressive, a tall, upright figure who excited a number of Australian critics, although I am told he struggles away from Adelaide's good wicket.

Peter Sleep, who was introduced into the Australian Test side eight years ago as a leg spinner, also held us up, having improved considerably as a batsman in recent years. Sleep was definitely more alert than his nickname 'Sounda' suggests, and overall I thought we had a good day despite South Australia's 305 for eight total at the end of it.

Saturday 1 November

Allan Lamb and James Whitaker were our saviours today after another shocking start that raised suggestions in the Australian media that we were suckers against left-arm pace bowling. It was hard not to agree after the way some of us got out.

Syd Parkinson, a chunky medium pacer, caused the speculation by claiming three wickets in his opening seven-over spell before adding another two later in the day. I was one of his first victims edging a catch behind after Chris Broad had been out leg before. Soon after my dismissal, Bill Athey dragged on a widish ball

after taking three boundaries off the previous four deliveries he had faced in the over. He was the unlucky one of the three.

That left us 38 for three, hardly the situation James Whitaker would have wanted, walking to the crease to make his first-class bow in Australia. He rose to the occasion magnificently, to the delight of his Adelaide fan club. He had spent two summers here playing second-grade cricket for Glenelg and had obviously proved a popular figure judging by the shouts whenever he played a good stroke. Allan Lamb was superb, watchful at first and then switching to all-out aggression in scoring our first first-class century of the tour, swiftly followed by Whitaker reaching three figures. Combined with a typical late dash from Ian Botham we were ahead by the end of the day with wickets to spare. The going appeared to be getting easier.

Sunday 2 November

Our prospects were looking even brighter by this evening. Again I was able to give the two spinners a long bowl when South Australia batted a second time. Once again it took the best of South Australia to have any chance of countering them, Phillips following his first-innings century by scoring 70 this time to hold us up for a while. I wondered whether he might be in contention for a Test place but I was told he would not have any chance for a while. Some months earlier he had been fined A$2,000 for describing the Australian selectors as 'idiots' when they left him out of the party that had recently toured India. The story sounded familiar. Fortunately our selectors appear more forgiving.

South Australian captain David Hookes is another who is said to be out of favour. After the way he made up for his first-innings duck by scoring a century today using his feet better than I have ever seen him, I left the ground hoping they would both remain black sheep for a few more months.

John Emburey got both of them in the end and finished the day with six for 102, bowling immaculately by the close when he was delivering the ball a little straighter and a little faster than at the start of his 38 overs. Phil Edmonds had the batsmen struggling just as hard yet finished the day wicketless. It is amazing how that can happen, two bowlers playing equally as well yet only one taking the honours. You win some, you lose some. We, of course, had been losing too many.

Monday 3 November

There was no question of our not winning this one today. At last a moment to savour. Handsomely done too, with five wickets to spare after being left to score 167. I knew we should win it but hardly dared think about it after the starts we had been making, especially being a batsman short with James Whitaker suffering from a touch of sunstroke following his long time in the middle two days ago. It was no better this time, Bill Athey's turn for a duck while I made only four. Fortunately

James Whitaker during his century against South Australia at Adelaide

Chris chipped in with his highest first-class score of the tour and Allan was still oozing supreme confidence. We got home with plenty of time to spare and I know I shall go to bed happy tonight.

England XI v South Australia
Played at Adelaide, Oct 31 Nov 1, 2, 3

S. Australia 305 for 8 dec (W. Phillips 116, G.A. Bishop 67,
P.R. Sleep 66*) and 269 (I.W. Hookes 104, W.B. Phillips 70,
J.E. Emburey 6 for 102)
England XI 407 (A.J. Lamb 105, J.J. Whitaker 108, I.T. Botham 70,
S.D.H. Parkinson 5 for 87) and 169 for 5 (B.C. Broad 63, A.J. Lamb 55)

England XI won by 5 wickets.

Tuesday 4 November

The win had given us a nice lift although it had done nothing to ease our basic problem, our continued failure to get a good start. This was the worry I discussed at length with Micky today as we moved on towards Perth and our final first-class warm-up game before the opening Test. Chris's innings was a bonus but he had looked good enough all along to secure one of the opening berths despite his shortage of runs until yesterday. The difficulty was in deciding between Wilf or Bill and we decided to let them fight it out in the one-day game against Western Australia Country XI in Kalgoorlie tomorrow.

There was one other concern although we tried not to let our worry show to the media. They had spotted the problem but we didn't want to encourage any special talk about it – the problem of the left-arm fast bowlers and the way we were falling to them quickly. Micky tried to take some of the heat out of the situation by saying it was only natural that we should have lost more wickets to left-arm pace bowlers than right-arm, simply because we had faced more of them in our two games. But it was a concern because we knew we were about to face two of the best in our next match: Western Australia's 6ft 8in Test bowler Bruce Reid and his colleague Chris Matthews.

Wednesday 5 November

I had decided to give the Kalgoorlie game a miss, staying behind in Perth yesterday while the bulk of the party moved on to Australia's gold mining centre. It would be my last chance to relax before the Test series started. Ian had arranged another fishing trip for the two of us but the weather cut up a little rough in the area

---

Bruce Reid, the dangerous left-arm bowler, who caused
early problems for England

where Great Britain's entry *White Crusader* was making a brave attempt to qualify for the final rounds of the America's Cup off Fremantle. We settled for a day on Rottnest Island just off the coast, a popular holiday picnic area for Perth residents. It was still nice to get away, the day made even more pleasant when I met up with the rest of the side in the evening and was told that Bill Athey had looked very impressive in scoring 124 in an easy victory. He was presented with a gold nugget for his innings, dug from a local mine by the cricket officials – a nice gesture.

England XI v Western Australia Country XI
Played at Kalgoorlie, Nov 5

England XI 293 for 5 (50 overs) (C.W.J. Athey 124)
W. Australia Country XI 176 for 9 (50 overs)

England XI won by 117 runs.

Thursday 6 November

Our batting collapses forced us to take one Test decision today a week earlier than we had wanted when we met to name the side to play Western Australia. That was to include Jack Richards as wicket-keeper.

Watching him and Bruce French so far, there had been little to choose between them as wicket-keepers but we felt that we needed Jack's extra batting skill to support batsmen who were still not coming off together. In the three years since first touring with England to India in 1981–82, Jack had concentrated on making himself a better batsman and had saved Surrey several times in recent years when in desperate trouble. By the end of the 1986 summer, he had five first-class centuries to his credit.

It was a very hard decision to take. We hadn't ruled Bruce completely out of the Test reckoning for Brisbane, although it would have been tough on him if we were forced to turn to him at the last moment when he would not have played cricket for 18 days apart from his Kalgoorlie appearance. The disappointment showed immediately on Bruce's face when I told him Jack would be playing tomorrow, when he clearly expected to get in again. Being captain has its rewards but it also has its unpleasant moments and this was one of them. Bruce is such a loyal and supportive person and I know my words hurt him.

Australia had named their First Test 12 yesterday and we were not too surprised. Most of the squad had been in India with the exception of Geoff Lawson who was making his way back after undergoing a back operation earlier in the year, correcting an injury similar to the one that threatened Dennis Lillee's career in the 1970s. Perhaps the one surprise was the omission of Craig McDermott in favour of Western Australia's Chris Matthews. It seemed the Australian selectors had been influenced by the media stories of our shortcomings against left-arm pace. It added extra spice to our coming match. We had expected them to include Bruce Reid and they had also recalled Victoria's bustling fast bowler Merv Hughes, a player we knew little about.

Friday 7 November

We were able to have a long look today at Australia's latest opening batsman, Geoff Marsh. Longer than I would have liked. But for him and three dropped catches, we would have had a good opening day against Western Australia who had won both their opening Sheffield Shield matches with the help of Somerset and England off-spinner Vic Marks. They had rested him from our match much to Ian's disappointment. He had promised he would hit Vic for six if the two had met. 'Everybody else does, so why shouldn't I?' he had told us.

Marsh dominated the first day after I had lost the toss, scoring a very patient century. It is easy to understand now why Australia have turned to him to provide stability at the top of their order in place of the rather suicidal batting Western Australia's captain Graeme Wood and South Australia's Andrew Hilditch had produced against us in 1985. Marsh is anything but a Kamikaze kid! He does have a tendency to play across the line early in his innings which offers the faster bowler a chance but once he is settled, he plays well within his limitations. He knows just what he can and can't do. He doesn't look capable of taking anybody apart but we all commented that he could prove a great irritant in the series ahead.

More worrying was our sloppy fielding with catches going down again, two of them in the slip area when Ian Botham was at fault, possibly losing them in the background. I changed places with him at second slip for a while to study the background but, unfortunately, the ball never came in my direction whilst I was there. I did make a mental note however to check the background again with the Second Test due to be played here. Micky did so also.

Saturday 8 November

The WACA ground witnessed a spectacle today that took everybody by surprise. Officials said it was the most astonishing sight they had seen for years. Unfortunately it was the weather that caused their astonishment and nothing we did on the field. There was time for about 30 minutes play shortly after lunch before an electrical storm, of the type that is common in the east but seldom in the west, returned to wash out play for the rest of the day.

It had struck first in the night ruining the prospect of any play before lunch but appeared to be fading into the distance when we arrived at the ground. No sooner had we started to play, than with a startling wind change it turned around and came in from the other side of the ground, streaks of lightning illuminating the sky all around as bright as Perth's new floodlighting system.

At least it gave me a chance to relax early and enjoy a meal out with Sue and Alan Mabbutt, relatives of my wife Elaine who have been in Australia for around 20 years. Most of the time I have been eating in the team hotel, taking advantage of the evenings by having chats with various players to see how they are feeling, making sure they are happy with the way things are going. Going out made a pleasant change, although I was still in bed early.

For the last two mornings I had been waking up prematurely, my body still tuned to Eastern States time which is three hours ahead of Perth. It is just one more example of the difficulty of this tour where we criss-cross Australia four times in the first five weeks. No sooner does the body get adjusted to a new place than we are on the move again, going through a time-zone change.

Sunday 9 November

Calamity, calamity again. Another depressing batting display. All out for 152 to finish 123 runs behind on first innings. I wonder when we are ever going to get a grip on things out here and I let my disappointment show in the dressing room. The worst aspect was David Gower getting out for a second-ball duck, not seeing a swinging yorker from Reid whose hand is above the sightscreen when he delivers. With his failure today our worry increased over getting a good start in the Test match.

There wasn't much about our batting to commend it. Chris played well until he lost his concentration again in the 30s. I must keep reminding him about the need to keep going. Ian thumped a few glorious boundaries. I suspect they were prompted by anger.

He had woken up in the bad mood this morning hearing that Somerset's members had backed the committee's decision to sack his West Indian friends Viv Richards and Joel Garner. Peter Lush again handled the situation well as the world waited to hear Ian's reaction at breakfast time. He allowed Ian to let off steam in private before attending a press conference when Ian had got most of his anger out of his system. He was much calmed by the time he reached the ground which allowed him to approach his cricket in a reasonable frame of mind, although still sizzling inside.

Monday 10 November

We were lucky to finish today without another defeat on our record, thanks to Graeme Wood. He carried on Western Australia's second innings until lunchtime by which time they were 330 runs ahead. If I had been in his position I would have declared 30 minutes earlier in an attempt to put us under pressure. I couldn't quite understand his approach later when he called off his victory hunt early although we had collapsed yet again with David making a pair. I was also out for a duck and it needed a very responsible 90-minute stay from Ian taking absolutely no risks to make sure we escaped with a draw from a very unsatisfactory warm-up game.

I tried to sound optimistic when facing the media at the end of the game but could not help feeling a little down by the time I returned to our hotel. Micky and I decided to hold a team meeting to try and get things straightened out before the Test match, asking the batsmen for a more patient and determined approach. Ian was very good at the meeting, virtually demanding that we should still return to Brisbane with our heads high, showing a confident front.

It was a fine, rallying cry but I didn't sleep easily. I kept going over the first four weeks in my mind wondering whether there was anything else that Micky and I should have done, but couldn't come up with anything. The lads were fit, looking very good in practice and it has got to be up to them as individuals to come up with the goods in the end. The warm-up games had not gone as well as I had wanted yet I felt we were not far away from being a good side.

England XI v Western Australia
Played at Perth, Nov 7, 8, 9 10

Western Australia 275 (G.R. Marsh 124, C.D. Matthews 56) and
207 for 8 dec (G.R. Marsh 63, G.M. Wood 53)
England XI 152 and 153 for 6 (A.J. Lamb 63)

Match Drawn.

Tuesday 11 November

I was more encouraged this morning on the long flight back to Brisbane via Sydney even though the newspapers had made unhappy reading. The Australian media had already written us off. Allan Border and his team had only to turn up to win the first Test, so it seemed. Yet I noticed a great improvement in the mood of our side. There was a general feeling of relief that the warm-up matches were over and now they could get down to concentrating on the serious business of winning Test matches. I shared their relief. Most of us had been on the go for ten months now with only a little break at the end of the summer at home. The warm-up games were necessary to help attain match fitness but they were hard to play.

It was a pity the mood was spoiled during the change-over of planes in Sydney where copies of the two Sydney evening newspapers came on board. One vitriolic attack on Ian Botham's character filed for an English newspaper trying to assess his next county had been quoted back and published with great glee under banner headlines. The article was certainly out of order as far as this tour was concerned. Nobody had tried harder than Ian, both on and off the field. He was upset and rightly so. By the time we arrived at the Brisbane hotel this evening, the mood of the party had blackened again, the other players fully on Ian's side.

The papers also contained out-of-context quote-backs from match reports in English papers referring to our Perth performance. The general theme was that we were heading for a hiding in Brisbane unless we bucked up our ideas, but one from Martin Johnson in the *Independent* went even further. He suggested we had three major problems – we couldn't bat, couldn't bowl, couldn't field. That provoked a 'we'll show them' response from the lads. Perhaps it was just the thing to get us fired up.

Wednesday 12 November

We took two important decisions today which, I hope, will help to bring everything into line for the opening Test in two days' time. The first concerned David Gower and a move I hoped would be just the fillip he needs after Perth – making him a tour selector.

All the time we had been in Australia David had seemed a man slightly on the outside, almost detached although he was with friends and admirers. It must have been a little difficult for him, wondering where he fitted in exactly. For the last two tours he had been the man in control and for the three previous years he had been one of the guiding lights as England's vice captain under Bob Willis. It must have been strange being just a player again. At home during the summer I had turned to him many times for advice on and off the field and I wanted his help now. Of the four of us on the selection panel, only John Emburey had done a complete tour of Australia, in 1978–79, although he had also been called in halfway through the 1979–80 tour when Geoff Miller was forced home early through injury.

I felt we needed the benefit of David's Australian experience to guide us on the selection panel and two days ago Peter Lush contacted Lord's to get the all-clear for David to join us. John Emburey said he would appreciate having an extra voice on the panel. He said he would have great difficulty arguing his own case to be included ahead of Phil Edmonds if we did decide to use only one spin bowler in a Test match. Above all, we felt it only right David should have some position of responsibility after all that he has done for English cricket. He did not hesitate when I put the offer to him.

The second decision was to call all the young players together this evening for a quiet chat. They must have been a little confused over what had happened and Micky and I thought it essential we should convince them that we were still going into the First Test with a great chance despite the way the newspapers were writing us off.

We did not want any of the hard work we had all put in to be wasted and explained that the poor performances against the state sides was just one of those things that happens as the pieces of the jigsaw come together. Many pieces are tried before the picture becomes complete and you can recognise the image. We were pleased with their response.

But I went to bed unhappy over one aspect of the tour. Word from home suggested that some English cricket writers were talking of us being a 'shambles'. That was a view expressed by two who had only recently arrived in Australia and had not been with us all the way through to see what we had done. I thought it unfair that we should be written off at home so comprehensively before we had played a Test match.

It was also unfair, I thought, that comparisons should have been drawn today between our approach at practice and that of the Australians. Our net wasn't as smooth as it should have been with various television and radio reporters swarming around the nets, shoving microphones to lips before we had a chance to take gloves or pads off. They got in the way and I was determined that would not happen again. They had, I gathered, left the Australians alone earlier in the morning, waiting until the net session was finished before approaching the Australian players for interviews, etc. It was going to be that way with us from now on, I decided.

There was also comment because the Australians returned to the Gabba ground for a second session after joining the rest of us for the official Benson & Hedges lunch to launch the Test series. Some media men seemed surprised that we had not gone back for a second session. The simple fact is that we had done our net training for the last five weeks and we did not need to have nets morning and afternoon. Bobby Simpson, the former Australian opening batsman and captain who was managing the Australian Test side, felt he did need two sessions because today was his first opportunity to work with the squad. He needed to get them together so they could get to know each other. It was not until they arrived at the nets this morning that Allan Border met Chris Matthews for the first time in his life. Astonishing, but a fact.

Thursday 13 November
David seems to be at the centre of most major decisions at the moment. It was the same when he joined us today to help select the team. This time the decision centred around his batting position in the team and I offered to go back to the number three position if he felt he would be happier going in at number five after his experiences so far. He agreed. It was something that had been on my mind for a week, ever since I had batted at number three against South Australia, although I had not been particularly successful. Allan Lamb had also suggested it. Micky and I had talked it over but we decided to say nothing, waiting to see how David fared in Perth. When he emerged from that game with a pair we decided to put my offer to him. David is such an essential part of the side we needed to make sure he was in the happiest frame of mind he could be to concentrate on the job in hand.

There were two other issues to be settled at the selection meeting. Whether Bill Athey or Wilf Slack should open with Chris Broad and whether Phil DeFreitas or Gladstone Small would be the third seam bowler if we decided to go into the Test with both spinners as seemed likely. Although the first-class returns of Wilf and Billy had not been very productive we finally opted for Billy because he had looked the more secure of the two in the time we had spent at the crease. He is a splendidly dedicated cricketer, always smart, with a marvellous attitude, a strong desire to succeed and prove a winner.

On the bowling front the choice was very narrow. On one hand we had the youth and extra pace of Daffy which might surprise one or two batsmen who had never seen him and could be deceived by his relaxed approach to the crease. He is faster than he looks. On the other hand we had to consider the experience and steadiness of Gladstone. I thought that he had probably bowled more good balls on the tour so far than any of the other pace bowlers without getting his just rewards. He certainly deserved more wickets than he had taken but I was also worried that he had been going for four runs an over, not bowling quite fast enough to keep the batsmen under control when the pitches became good. We decided on Daffy which meant we were including two new caps with Jack Richards taking over as wicket-keeper.

We finished the day by having a team dinner in the hotel, something I was very keen on. On some recent tours this tradition has been abandoned but I insisted we should start the series by having one at least. I felt that in Australia where there are so many other attractions, good restaurants and friendly people with invitations to dinner, it would be easy for the team to become fragmented, groups going their separate ways. The dinner was the chance to bring everybody back together again, remind them what we are here to do, talk about the opposition and concentrate the mind on the job ahead. The response was excellent and I certainly approached the First Test happier than I had been three days earlier. I thought we could do well despite what the critics were saying. There was certainly not a defeatist atmosphere at the dinner, more one of confidence.

The only part of the day that had disturbed me was finding the Australians had booked the nets in the morning. The net facilities at the Gabba are not large, two nets only being set up on the outfield. We had to wait until the Australians had finished in the nets before we had a chance to use them. This is something that does not happen at home. As the host country we always offer the opposition first choice of the nets. Generally speaking, it suits everybody for them to have the nets in the morning and for us to use them in the afternoon. But they do have the choice. We were not given that choice here. Sometimes I wonder whether we are too obliging when we are at home.

The two captains, Allan Border and I, testing our strength before the battle begins in earnest

Victory against the odds

Friday 14 November

The lads in the dressing room told me my face looked a picture of misery in a television close-up when I lost the toss. I wish they had shown a close-up of my face at the end of the day. I was wearing a smile as wide as Sydney harbour with us finishing on 189 for two after being put in. It was a marvellous day.

In fact I wasn't that miserable over losing the toss, which is a very public occasion over here, unlike at home where it is conducted privately by the two captains with, perhaps, the groundsman hovering a few yards away awaiting instructions. In Australia Channel 9 television cameras are everywhere. There is one to greet Allan Border and myself in the middle, along with former England captain Tony Greig complete with microphone to intrude on the moment and carry out interviews.

The toss winner is always the first to be interviewed about his intention and

Australian cameramen surround us before the
start of the First Test

hopes and I was left in the background to reflect on what it all meant. We suspected that Allan would slip us in with the wicket having a fair covering of grass. He had done so when winning the toss for Queensland against us, winning the match. He had also done so when winning the toss against Tasmania – and found himself facing a 500-plus first-innings total. I hadn't quite made up my mind what we should do if I had won the toss. I was tempted to put Australia in but I did not expect the pitch to be as helpful as Allan obviously did and thought it would be a very good track after the first hour or so. I wasn't unhappy not having to make the decision. I wasn't too unhappy about us batting first either, despite that close-up shot of my face on television.

We had been a little behind schedule going out for the toss with the Australians obviously having some trouble working out their final 11 before it was announced that they were leaving out Geoff Lawson, their most experienced fast bowler. It caused a few raised eyebrows in our dressing room. It left them with a very inexperienced pace attack, Bruce Reid having played in just eight Test matches, Merv Hughes one and Chris Matthews making his Test début. We had no difficulty settling on playing both John Emburey and Phil Edmonds, leaving Gladstone Small as 12th man. We thought that if we did fail to make a new-ball breakthrough, John could contain as well as any pace bowler, if not better.

The inexperience of the Australian faster bowlers showed, fortunately for us. Nerves must have played a part as well but none of them bowled a consistent line although Reid improved as the day wore on. Chris Matthews was never sure where the ball was going. Hughes was little better although clearly the fastest bowler and when he did get it right, produced a very good ball. Despite that we still could not get a start and I was to find myself at the wicket with the game less than an hour old.

Chris Broad was the batsman to fall. He had been beaten a couple of times by good deliveries from Hughes but was starting to look sound when he suffered a momentary lapse of concentration against the left-arm bowling of Reid and edged an away-swinger behind. Looking at it on television later I noticed that he wasn't quite getting across to cover that delivery and made a note to talk to him later at an opportune moment.

It was a tricky time for us. Bill was fighting bravely without looking totally convincing during the opening overs. When I joined him at the wicket I told him it was essential that the two of us should stay there until lunch and for at least an hour afterwards if we could. We were to do nothing fancy, just a solid, workmanlike and professional job in seeing off the faster bowlers while the pitch was offering them some assistance. Bill did his job well. There were a few words exchanged now and again whenever Hughes beat him outside the off stump. The Victorian fast bowler has a wonderful Edwardian walrus-type moustache which makes him look ten years older than his 25 years. He's quite an aggressive character on the field as all fast bowlers should be, with the habit of glaring at the batsman, hands on hips, at the end of his follow through when he has bowled a good ball. He also mutters a few words suggesting the batsman is the luckiest human being in the world and I

Ian Botham in top form during his 138 in the First Test

James Whitaker during his century against South Australia

Bill Athey narrowly missed a hundred – out for 96 in the Second Test

Hitting out before we decided caution was the best approach

Chris Broad continues his prolific form – 162 in the Second Test

Merv Hughes, fastest of the Australian bowlers

was a little concerned once when I saw Bill's lips moving in reply. I didn't want Hughes upsetting Bill's concentration and started to intercede until I heard that Bill was taking care of himself quite nicely. It was Hughes and not Bill who was getting upset. Bill answered Hughes' verbal offensive by touching his forelock rather like a country yokel talking to the local squire and saying 'sorry sir, sorry sir'. Poor Hughes looked even more puzzled.

The only real alarm we had was when I edged an attempted drive against Hughes which Steve Waugh might have got to in the gully although it would have been a marvellous catch if he had completed it, high to his left. We were then at a stage where I could afford to open out a little, Bill having grown in confidence and looking very solid.

We turned our second-wicket partnership into three figures before I fell with the total on 116, missing a drive against Hughes when the ball seamed off the wicket, caught my back pad and was diverted onto my wicket. I was quite surprised to learn afterwards that of the nine fours I had struck in my half century, eight of them had been taken off Chris Matthews as though I had made a deliberate attempt to take the new Australian bowler apart. That had not been my intention.

My dismissal brought in Allan Lamb and he looked very secure right from the start as he joined Bill in seeing us through to the premature close for bad light without further loss. They had to cope with a couple of breaks through rain, which disturbed me when the Gabba groundstaff looked some time in getting the wicket covered. Each time Bill and Allan went out to bat again I watched anxiously to see if the wicket had been freshened up at all but neither was in any trouble.

By the time the light was bad enough to call a halt Bill had scored 76, and I'm sure he would have got a century if we had managed to play the full six hours but the progress we made provided us with our best opening day in a Test since the first day against Australia at The Oval in 1985. I dined well.

Saturday 15 November.
As satisfying as the first day had been, today was even better despite a first 20 minutes that threatened to bring us down when we lost both overnight batsmen without a run being added. It was Ian Botham's day, living up to the promise he had personally made to Micky and myself when we spoke to him about his attitude and approach to the tour two months earlier. His century was a magnificent effort. He was responsible for producing a first-innings total of 456, which gave us a chance of making Australia follow on, a total that was boosted in the final 30 minutes when Daffy DeFreitas marked his Test début with the wicket of Australian opener David Boon. Yet it had been built on rather shaky ground.

The first ball from Hughes on the second day gave us a severe jolt when Allan Lamb was given out leg before. Worse was to follow four overs later when Bill Athey got an inside edge against Chris Matthews and Australian wicket-keeper Tim Zoehrer was able to change direction swiftly enough to take the catch down the leg side.

With such a double blow I couldn't think of two better players in the world to take over in the situation than David Gower and Ian, although David was still below his best. He might have fallen before he had scored when he drove rather loosely against Chris Matthews and Hughes almost brought off a great catch at third slip. Many people put it down as a drop but I was sitting right behind Hughes and I thought he did marvellously well even to get a hand to it, diving to his right about shoulder high. The ball went like a bullet. What did surprise me was Hughes being in the third-slip position when he was sharing the attack.

Against Western Australia a week earlier DeFreitas had dropped a third-slip chance, a rather easy one. He got the blame for it from the media, but I was the one at fault. I should never have put him there when I had a couple of good slip

Ian Botham during his brilliant 138 in Brisbane

catchers in the field, and I suspect Allan Border was kicking himself for his lapse in having Hughes in a close-catching position when he is normally an outfielder.

David continued to have a little luck at the start of his innings. Ian, however, was as safe as Fort Knox right from the start in their partnership which took the score from 189 for four to 316 for five before David was out, pulling a short ball fiercely to mid-wicket.

Only once during their partnership did Ian's determination waver, when he got carried away a little against Hughes and the new ball. He sent three of the first four balls crashing to the boundary and started to get carried away. He aimed yet another booming drive against the fifth ball, missing completely although very near to getting a thin edge. It prompted David to walk down the wicket and say to him, 'I think I should tell you exactly what Gatt is saying in the dressing room at this very moment but perhaps I'd better not'. It worked. Botham met the last ball of the over with a perfectly straight defensive bat and never wavered again on his path to his century, only the third scored by an English batsman at the Gabba.

He lost two other partners before he reached three figures, including Jack Richards who was out for nought on his Test début. I felt very sorry for Jack. We had put him under pressure by selecting him for his batting and I knew that had sparked a great deal of sympathy at home for Bruce French. Jack's duck would bring up the whole issue again.

John Emburey was out before Ian found the partner he needed in Daffy. Ian had taken a great interest in Daffy's progress on the tour, spending a long time talking to him and encouraging him, one reason why we had teamed them up as room-mates twice on the tour. Daffy had also taken to phoning Peter Willey back in Leicestershire for extra words of encouragment, saying he always felt better when he had talked to Will. Whatever was said, it worked today as he stayed with Botham during a 92-run partnership for the eighth wicket that proved vital to our cause.

It was helped by a fine piece of sportsmanship by the Australian players when Daffy had made only three. He had started to walk, believing he had been caught by Allan Border standing widish at second slip. There was no question that Daffy had edged the ball but it was always going down, forcing Border to dive forward in an attempt to complete the catch. He finished flat out but held the ball up, saying immediately that he wasn't sure whether the catch had been clean. By then umpire Mel Johnson had already raised his finger and Daffy had started to leave the crease when Ian – at the bowler's end – turned to Mel Johnson and said 'How can you give him out when Border says he isn't sure whether the catch was clean?' It prompted Daffy to stay while Johnson consulted square-leg umpire Tony Crafter who said his view had been blocked by wicket-keeper Tim Zoehrer, and it took Greg Ritchie, who had been fielding in the covers, to clear up the issue when he said he thought the ball had bounced – a view confirmed by slow-motion television replays. The players in the middle were not to know that, of course, and Ritchie's intervention resulted in the Australians withdrawing the appeal allowing Daffy to stay there for another 37 runs.

Test debutant Phil DeFreitas

The decision helped Ian reach his century, going on to make 138 before he was caught at long leg, hooking. His total was the highest individual Test score by an England batsman on the ground, beating Maurice Leyland's 126 in 1936–7. It was a superb performance off 174 balls with 13 fours and four sixes. We were able to get the Australians in for an hour on the second night.

That was a bonus, especially when Boon attempted to punish a shortish ball from Daffy just before the close only to be caught at mid-wicket, forcing Australia to send in Zoehrer as the nightwatchman. We had got them on the run.

Sunday 16 November

It gets better every day. This time it was the bowlers who took all the honours, everyone playing their part to perfection. Micky had spent a lot of time stressing to the faster bowlers that they had to bowl a consistent line around off stump, giving the batsmen nothing to hit. They did just that with Graham Dilley extremely fast as well as accurate. John Emburey was at his most mean, showing superb control and Phil Edmonds did everything I asked of him to perfection as well as chipping in with the vital wicket of Allan Border. There was never any question of not enforcing the follow-on when they were all out 208 runs behind.

There were a couple of periods during the day – when Geoff Marsh and Tim Zoehrer turned their second stand into 50 and later when Greg Ritchie and Greg Matthews were together for a long time – when nothing really happened. Yet at no time did I ever feel that the game was drifting away. I always felt something was about to happen. Each time it did.

I was also very happy about the field settings. The accuracy of the bowlers allowed me to set a field that was always attacking yet never gave the batsmen unearned runs, something that can be very demoralising. When the batsmen did occasionally manage to find the boundary, there was generally a large element of risk in their stroke.

I decided before the start that I would bring John into the attack early, having watched Australia bowl on the first two days. I felt that Allan Border had used his faster men in too long spells with the result that they tired quickly and became even more wayward after bowling seven or eight overs. My intention was to get John to act as a full stop at one end, using Graham, Ian and Daffy in short, attacking bursts at the other. There was enough in the wicket to encourage the faster bowlers with some movement off the seam. We had the bonus of John turning a few early on which put doubt in the minds of the Australian batsmen, allowing him to dominate them completely in bowling his 34 overs for just 66 runs. He didn't take a wicket but earned three or four for the other bowlers.

In terms of figures, the bowling honours went to Graham Dilley taking five wickets in an innings for the first time in Test cricket. How thoroughly he deserved them. He made the initial breakthrough in the morning, having the stubborn Zoehrer leg before, followed by DeFreitas dismissing Dean Jones in a similar fashion. Two wickets in the morning session in exchange for 84 runs was a fair exchange as far as I was concerned.

By the first interval Emburey had settled in well, never really giving the batsmen any chance of breaking free, a domination he held over Border for an hour as the Australian captain struggled in single figures. The important break had come before then when Dilley produced a great outswinger that found the edge of Marsh's bat to give Jack Richards a catch behind, but still the vital wicket

Graham Dilley, during his five-wicket haul

was that of Border's. When he is at the wicket, the Australians always look more confident. Phil Edmonds removed him for me although Emburey was really responsible.

He had reeled off 22 overs in succession for the cost of just 45 runs when I gave him a break and brought on Phil, largely in an effort to speed the coming of the second new ball. Border saw the switch as an opportunity to attempt to break free after being completely bogged down, but his first attacking gesture in Phil's opening over was to drive a catch to backward point which DeFreitas held, although he admitted he did not see the ball until the last moment. He did not have time to get his hands up to catch it before it thumped into his chest. Fortunate, perhaps, but Border had gone leaving Australia on 159 for five. I knew then we would make them follow on. When I asked Phil to take over from John I explained it was to quicken the arrival of the second new ball and told him to give me 11 overs for very little. His 11 overs cost 11 runs with the wicket of Border into the bargain. It was delightful stuff so that when the second new ball was due Australia had made only 191 runs for their five wickets.

Despite the control of John and Phil, I had no hesitation in taking the new ball immediately which opened the way for Graham Dilley's finest effort. Greg Ritchie had been playing the spin quite well after several early alarms, but he had no chance with another superb delivery from Graham which turned him round, edging a catch to gully. We had one end open. The Australians were never to close it.

Graham struck again in his next over, having Steve Waugh caught behind for a duck, two wickets that inspired Ian into greater effort claiming Chris Matthews and Merv Hughes, leaving last man Bruce Reid to partner Greg Matthews. They needed another 18 runs to avoid the follow-on at that stage and it got a little tight as Dilley and Botham tired.

They had been bowling for an hour with the new ball by then and I did suggest to Graham that he might like to take a rest. With four wickets to his credit and Reid in his sights he looked at me as though I had gone berserk. I knew I wasn't going to get the ball off him. He summoned up one more effort only for me to drop Reid at second slip. I had moved a little closer seeing the way Reid batted, afraid that an edge would not reach. This time the edge was thick and firm. I managed to get a hand to it, palming it up and behind where Ian made a good effort to take the rebound. I wondered for a moment whether that miss might cost us the chance of winning the game. Fortunately Reid duly obliged with a catch behind soon after and I had the honour of asking Allan Border to bat again tonight although there was time for only one over. With the rest day coming up I was able to enjoy a few beers this evening – albeit Australian ones!

Monday 17 November
I just couldn't get to sleep tonight. I can't remember when I have been so keyed up. Even dinner with an old friend, Ray Gallian who had come up from Sydney, failed to relax me although I stayed up late chatting beyond my normal bedtime

before a match. My mind just would not switch off as I went through the possible alternatives should we not make an early breakthrough tomorrow. We were so close, a great opportunity to go one ahead in the series, I wanted every eventuality covered.

I had given myself the rare luxury of a lie-in during the morning before playing 18 holes of golf in the afternoon along with Peter Lush, Gladstone Small and Neil Foster. Some of the other players used the chance to visit Queensland's famous Gold Coast, enjoying the sun and the marvellous seafood. Three others had stayed in. Knowing the amount of work they would be expected to do on the fourth day, Ian Botham, Graham Dilley and Daffy DeFreitas had all opted to spend the day resting up. It was not until 5.30 in the afternoon that Graham finally got out of his bed. Nobody had insisted they should stay in. It was entirely their decision but it showed the determination among the team to succeed.

Despite that determination it was ages before I dropped off to sleep. I couldn't quite believe that we were so well placed and felt something must go wrong.

Tuesday 18 November

It didn't. I was hoping that we might have finished the fourth day with seven Australian wickets but was quite happy to settle for the five that we did get, considering how well the wicket was playing and the way the wind had turned around which meant that the bowlers had to bowl from the opposite ends. They would have been happier bowling from the ends where they had taken the wickets and established control on Sunday.

Today's effort was a thoroughly professional job. We kept the batsmen on a tight rein, chipping in with the wickets whenever they attempted to break free, with only Geoff Marsh having the concentration and the patience to see it through, making a controlled century before the end of the day.

I would sooner have got him out, of course, but there was never any danger of him taking us apart and dictating terms, so I let him get on quietly with his job while attacking at the other end. This time John Emburey got his just reward for his efforts with the support of DeFreitas although Daffy did stray a little in the middle of the day. He became a little too ambitious in seeking wickets and I had to remind him to concentrate on bowling the off-stump line, pitching the ball up and allowing the batsmen to bring about their own downfall in their frustration.

The first hour of the day belonged to us when Ian Botham managed to get one through the guard of David Boon to win a leg-before appeal, and then John Emburey had Dean Jones stumped. During the rest day Australia's cricket manager Bobby Simpson had said that his batsmen must try and be more positive playing against the spin bowlers and Jones had started as though he intended to take them on. I was quite happy with him adopting that approach for I thought there would be only one winner. I was proved correct when Jones suddenly went down the wicket against John, who saw him coming, producing a faster and shorter ball. Jones was stumped by at least a couple of yards, a good stumping because Jack Richards did not see the ball until it went under Jones' bat.

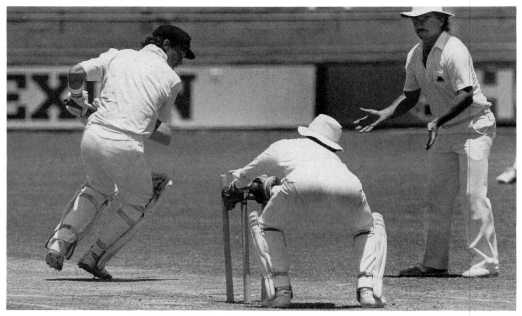

Dean Jones is stumped by Jack Richards

The second hour before lunch belonged to Australia in the partnership I probably feared most – Allan Border teaming up with Marsh. They were the two batsmen I felt could wreck our plans, the two with the patience and wit to survive for a long time and Border looked far more settled than he had done in the first innings. By lunch they had carried Australia to 90 for two without looking in any trouble.

We knew it was essential to split them as quickly as possible and we had our stroke of luck after lunch when Border just failed to get on top of one from John as he played forward defensively leaving Allan Lamb at silly mid-off to take the catch via pad and glove. It was the breakthrough we needed to go on for victory.

Of the Australian batsmen, Greg Ritchie had looked the most secure against the spin bowlers and Border's wicket was the only one we were to earn during the afternoon, despite switching the bowlers around, trying the spinners from different ends and then attempting a quick thrust with pace. None of it worked and I decided the new ball had to be the weapon.

It worked, although Graham Dilley was not as sharp with the new ball as I had hoped. I gave him just three overs before deciding to give DeFreitas a chance with the wind, a move that saw him have Ritchie leg before playing across the line to end a troublesome 113-run stand of almost three hours. We were on our way again. By this evening the Australians had moved into the lead but we had captured another wicket with Dilley taking a return catch against Greg Matthews in a final fling that just turned the day our way.

The lads were a little quiet in the dressing room at the close. I think they were

John Emburey clean bowls Stephen Waugh

disappointed we had not taken more Australian wickets. They were all very much exhausted too. It had taken considerable effort and concentration in chipping away for the five wickets we had captured and I was very pleased the way they kept going particularly when Marsh and Ritchie had spent three hours at the crease.

Once again sleep did not come easily. I was 90 per cent certain that we had the game in the bag. It was just that 10 per cent doubt that kept nagging away, keeping me awake until gone midnight.

Wednesday 19 November

I need not have worried. It was long after midnight before I went to sleep tonight. But that was caused by our celebrations after going ahead in the series, a match the Australians were convinced they were going to win when it had started six days earlier. I think they had been taken in by the Australian media predictions that we were a bunch of no-hopers.

For the first 30 minutes nothing had happened. I had even been forced to abandon the attacking field I had set first thing when Steve Waugh played a number of attractive strokes to demonstrate why the Australian selectors have continued to back him although he has scored only one Test half century. I had already signalled to John Emburey that I was bringing him into the attack at the end of the next over from DeFreitas when the Leicestershire bowler dismissed century-maker Marsh making one seam in off the wicket. At the end of the previous over Daffy had said he thought he could do Marsh that way and it worked

59

perfectly. It was the breakthrough we wanted and within 30 minutes their innings had ended, five wickets going down for 39 runs with John Emburey taking three of them for two runs in 23 deliveries. He had struck in his first over when bowling Steve Waugh to gain his 100th Test wicket. I was delighted for him.

That left us needing 75 to win and I was determined there was not going to be any messing about, especially after Bill Athey had fallen to a third-slip catch with only six runs on the board. With so much time to spare I had seen too many sides nervously push for the runs and end up in trouble. I didn't want that to happen.

My first three scoring strokes were all boundaries and I was aiming for another when I whipped the ball to square leg to be caught. It was a short innings but I wanted to give us some impetus so that by the time we reached lunch the victory was virtually assured. I didn't want the team sitting around still wondering what might happen and I think it worked.

We still lost Allan Lamb before victory was confirmed by seven wickets. Chris Broad produced the stroke of the day, for me, when he stood up on his toes and cracked Merv Hughes magnificently to the extra-cover boundary for the winning run. Within two minutes the cork was off the first bottle of champagne in the dressing room, champagne the management had swiftly arranged.

The Australian dressing room next door was silent, the door kept shut with Allan Border refusing to make any appearance at first. I saw him briefly at the end of the match to say 'thanks for the game'. He was very upset – and rightly so. He has done so much for Australian cricket even if most of it has been in a defensive vein attempting to hold the side together, fighting against defeat, yet I felt he was cruelly attacked by some of the Australian media. They had not helped him by writing us off before the start of the match, which made Australia's defeat look even worse in the eyes of the Australian public.

Allan was too fraught to attend the immediate after-match television interviews, sending in his vice captain David Boon to collect the losers' cheque and I understand he was snappy and broody when finally persuaded to meet the Australian media.

In contrast our dressing room door was wide open to everybody for we knew just how important the victory was for us. Before the series we had viewed Brisbane and Perth as the danger Test matches because we felt both centres contained wickets that might have suited the Australian bowlers better. Now we had triumphed on the ground where the Australians had expected victory, especially after their confidence-boosting tour of India. We had shattered them.

So many of us had registered firsts with the victory. It was my first Test win as England's captain, the first time Chris Broad had finished on a winning England side in seven Test matches. I don't think anybody was more delighted than our physiotherapist Laurie Brown who was sampling his first England Test victory, although he had been with us for 11 Test matches. It was a wonderful way for Jack Richards and Phil DeFreitas to launch their Test careers and, astonishingly, it was only the second time Graham Dilley had been on a winning England side in 23 Test matches.

The two faces of captaincy: Allan Border looks drained while we celebrate victory in the First Test

The celebrations were long and noisy. Two hours after the victory we were still at the ground and there were more drinks from well-wishers waiting for us when we arrived back in our hotel for the evening, by which time the telegrams had started to arrive. I was particularly touched by the one from Tony Brown, the Somerset chief executive who had been our manager in the West Indies earlier in the year.

The celebration dinner was back in the Chinese restaurant that evening along with the management team before returning to the hotel, where I discovered Peter May, chairman of the selectors, had phoned with a message saying 'Congratulations. Delighted.' I don't think Peter Lush will mind me commenting that he looked distinctly wobbly when he left the bar. That applied to the rest of us, too. As Micky Stewart said in the dressing room some hours earlier, 'I shall be disappointed if everybody doesn't have a headache in the morning'.

FIRST TEST MATCH

Woolloongabba, Brisbane, November 14, 15, 16, 18, 19

ENGLAND		Runs	Mins	Balls	4s		Runs	Mins	Balls	4s
B.C. Broad	c Zoehrer b Reid	8	33	35	—	not out	35	87	62	6
C.W.J. Athey	c Zoehrer b Matthews, C.	76	291	189	7	c Waugh b Hughes	1	13	10	—
*M.W. Gatting	b Hughes	61	147	118	11	c Matthews, G. b Hughes	12	15	15	3
A.J. Lamb	lbw b Hughes	40	93	80	7	lbw b Reid	9	21	23	—
D.I. Gower	c Ritchie b Matthews, C.	51	146	91	6	not out	15	32	28	2
I.T. Botham	c Hughes b Waugh	138	251	174	13*					
†C.J. Richards	b Matthews, C.	0	6	4	—					
J.E. Emburey	c Waugh b Hughes	8	41	31	1					
P.A.J. DeFreitas	c Matthews, C. b Waugh	40	75	71	6					
P.H. Edmonds	not out	9	14	10	1					
G.R. Dilley	c Boon b Waugh	0	5	8	—					
Extras	(b3, lb19, nb3)	25	*Plus 4 sixes			(b2, nb3)	5			
		456				(3 wkts)	77			

Fall: 15, 116, 198, 198, 316, 324, 351, 443, 451, 456. 6, 25, 40.

Bowling: Reid 31-4-86-1, Hughes 36-7-134-3, Matthews, C. 35-10-95-3, Waugh 21-3-76-3, Matthews, G. 11-2-43-0.

Matthews, C. 4-0-11-0, Hughes 5.3-0-28-2, Reid 6-1-20-1, Matthews, G. 7-1-16-0.

AUSTRALIA		Runs	Mins	Balls	4s			Runs	Mins	Balls	4s
G.R. Marsh	c Richards b Dilley	56	204	159	8	(2)	b DeFreitas	110	393	311	12
D.C. Boon	c Broad b DeFreitas	10	46	32	2	(1)	lbw b Botham	14	34	22	—
†T.J. Zoehrer	lbw b Dilley	38	89	86	5	(8)	not out	16	29	23	3
D.M. Jones	lbw DeFreitas	8	40	32	—	(3)	st Richards b Emburey	18	26	24	2
*A.R. Border	c DeFreitas b Edmonds	7	66	47	—	(4)	c Lamb b Emburey	23	71	78	2
G.M. Ritchie	c Edmonds b Dilley	41	118	115	4*	(5)	lbw b DeFreitas	45	175	164	2 *
G.R.J. Matthews	not out	56	165	115	5	(6)	c & b Dilley	13	30	26	2
S.R. Waugh	c Richards b Dilley	0	7	5	—	(7)	b Emburey	28	53	41	3
C.D. Matthews	c Gatting b Botham	11	53	34	1		lbw b Emburey	0	1	2	—
M.G. Hughes	b Botham	0	1	2	—		b DeFreitas	0	8	7	—
B.A. Reid	c Richards b Dilley	3	22	7	—		c Broad b Emburey	2	10	7	—
Extras	(b2, lb8, w2, nb6)	18					(b5, lb6, nb2)	13			
		248	*Plus 1 six					282	*Plus 1 six		

Fall: 27, 97, 114, 126, 159, 198, 204, 239, 239, 248. 24, 44, 92, 205, 224, 262, 266, 266, 275, 282.

Bowling: DeFreitas 16-5-32-2, Dilley 25.4-7-68-5, Emburey 34-11-66-0, Edmonds 12-6-12-1, Botham 16-1-58-2, Gatting 1-0-2-0.

Botham 12-0-34-1, Dilley 19-6-47-1, Emburey 42.5-15-80-5, DeFreitas 17-2-62-3, Edmonds 24-8-46-0, Gatting 2-0-2-0.

Toss won by Australia
Man of the Match: I.T. Botham

Test debuts: C.D. Matthews (Aus), P.A.J. DeFreitas, C.J. Richards (Eng)
Umpires: A.R. Crafter & M.W. Johnson

ENGLAND WON BY 7 WICKETS

Disappointment at Perth

Thursday 20 November

After last night's celebrations, we were not as well prepared for today as we might have been – another horror flight on a small aircraft that upset us all as we hopped from Brisbane to Newcastle via a landing at Surfer's Paradise. It might have been alright if the plane had been on time but it was held up for an hour by bad weather in Sydney.

By the time we climbed aboard some 90 minutes late, those storms had moved up the coast and we flew straight into them on the first leg which was only 30 minutes' flying. It was not sufficient time for the pilot to get above the thick cloud layer, so we spent the entire period in the clouds being buffetted left and right, up and down. One poor stewardess hit her head on the ceiling during one sudden drop and it was impossible to serve tea or coffee. Even our bravest fliers admitted they were shaken when the plane put down in Surfer's Paradise.

The final leg to Newcastle was a little better although the weather was still poor which left us wondering what the wicket would be like for the start of tomorrow's four-day state game against New South Wales, the Sheffield Shield champions. Normally the match would have been played on the Sydney Test ground but that was required for the visit of the Pope.

It was disappointing to find that we were not playing in Sydney, which meant that we would not get a taste of the Test ground until we arrived there for the final Test in the middle of January. Newcastle does not have much to commend it and the New South Wales players did not really fancy playing an important fixture on a country ground with little or no atmosphere. Newcastle does boast a couple of nice beaches, one immediately opposite the team hotel but there we had another disappointment. It had been taken over for one of Australia's major surfing championships the weekend we were staying. It was too cold to bathe anyway.

Friday 21 November

Our fears about the pitch were confirmed this morning. It was damp at the start and not really fit and I thought we might be in trouble when John Emburey lost the toss and Dirk Wellham, the New South Wales captain, put us in. I had decided to take the match off, having worked out it would be the last game I could miss before the tour ended. Unfortunately the recent rain had ruined the practice nets so I had nothing to distract me from the events in the middle.

We did manage to have one bright moment just before the start when an elderly local resident produced a picture of the 1928–29 England party and asked us if we could indentify the players. We told him we did not recognise anybody apart from Walter Hammond but we pointed out Micky Stewart and told him he would know because he was on the tour. Micky's face was a picture when the chap approached him and asked him 'Would you mind identifying your colleagues on this tour?'

Bruce French enjoyed himself today as well. He finished top scorer with an undefeated 38 when we were bowled out for 197, once hooking Geoff Lawson superbly off his nose to the boundary during his two-hour stay. With Neil Foster and Gladstone Small also in good nick with the bat, the last three wickets took the score from 106 for eight to 197. Bruce was even more delighted by the end of the day when he took a very smart stumping as John Emburey snapped up two New South Wales wickets. If New South Wales had batted first I doubt whether they would have reached three figures against John on a wicket offering extravagant turn before lunch.

Saturday 22 November
With the practice wickets still unfit I managed to get in a round of golf today to keep the exercise going, only to meet with a great disappointment when I returned to the hotel. We had been doing very nicely when I had left in the morning and I later heard at the golf club that New South Wales had been bowled out for 181 giving us a 16-run lead. I had not heard any progress since then and was greeted with the news that we had been reduced to 66 for nine at the close by some very tight line and length bowling by Mike Whitney and Dave Gilbert.

Several of the players were in the lobby when I got back and they were a little dazed by it all. Bill Athey told me, 'We all tried, nobody was doing anything silly when they got out yet the wickets kept on falling'. I suppose there was some consolation in the fact they had fallen to Test bowlers rather than some young unknown. I could smell trouble ahead, however.

Sunday 23 November
My instinct was right. Before we actually went down by eight wickets in suffering our second defeat of the tour by a state side, the media were looking for answers with the second Test against Australia starting in five days time, but I was not able to help them.

They expected me to be concerned and seemed surprised when I said I was not. Concern was not the right word. I was disappointed in our performance but it was hard for the players to be motivated after their success in Brisbane, especially on a ground containing so little atmosphere. Perth seemed a million miles away and I knew we had plenty of time to get Newcastle well out of the system.

If anybody should have been concerned it was the Australian selectors. After leaving Geoff Lawson out of the first Test side where his experience was badly missed, they were watching him closely in this game, but he was not particularly impressive even in the first innings. When batting in their first innings he had taken a blow on his right arm from Gladstone Small and had suggested to Wellham that Gilbert and Whitney should share the new ball when we batted a second time. They not only shared it, they rolled us over, Lawson bowling only four overs, giving him no opportunity to show the selectors whether he was fully fit.

I left the ground soon after the finish to drive to Sydney with manager Peter Lush and Graham Dilley so that we could study some alternative accommodation that had been offered to us for our stay there during the one-day international series. That was our excuse to the others anyway. In fact, we drove down because none of us wanted to climb on a small plane again. It was a very pleasant drive, made even more so by the absence of sick bags!

England XI v New South Wales
Played at Newcastle, Nov 21, 22, 23

England XI 197 and 82 (M.R. Whitney 5 for 39)
New South Wales 181 and 99 for 2

New South Wales won by 8 wickets.

Monday 24 November

The light aircraft flight turned out to be very uneventful, or so the players told me when I caught up with them at Sydney Airport. The whole day had been, apart from Ian Terence Botham celebrating his 31st birthday. He started by inviting a group to lunch in Newcastle and was to finish it on our arrival in Perth by attending a party with Elton John who was in the city to stage three concerts. It was just as well Ian had not counted on celebrating his birthday on the long haul from Sydney to Perth. Before the journey was an hour old, the airline had run out of wine – which 'Both' would not have appreciated – there was none left to go with our dinner on the flight.

It was another of those journeys where we ran into the time-zone problems. By the time we got to our hotel in Perth it was a little after 8.30 pm and the hotel was coming alive with evening visitors, yet it was midnight Sydney time. You felt a little silly going to bed so early local time but the need for sleep won in my case! It has been the quietest day on the tour.

Tuesday 25 November

It seems we have caused a little stir again by our decision to give the players a free day – apart from those who had not played in Newcastle – following our three-day defeat by New South Wales.

The media expected us to be hard at it and I had to explain that three days in the nets on the Perth ground would not have helped us prepare for the Test match on Friday. If I had insisted on three days of nets I know the players would have been bored by the Thursday. I preferred to let them have today off on the promise that they would work hard for two days, Thursday in particular, to apply the edge for the actual Test match. I'm not sure I convinced all my media questioners.

Wednesday 26 November

One worry we could have done without today. John Emburey volunteered to help out in the nets yesterday when Graham Dilley, Allan Lamb, Jack Richards, Phil DeFreitas and I had some practice to make up for missing Newcastle, and trapped a nerve in the elbow on his right arm. It is quite painful and we had to tell him to take the rest of the morning off when it hurt during catching practice on the wide and immaculate Perth outfield. It is a blow, although Laurie Brown is working on it and says it should clear by Friday.

It has been another pleasant, relaxing day. Last night several of us attended Elton John's first concert in Perth, a masterly show which he dominates for almost four hours. The first half of the show is pure Elton with his own support group but for the second half he has the Melbourne Symphony Orchestra with him: it is a fascinating mixture. You have to admire his energy and style. The rest of the team went this evening and even Peter Lush and Mickey Stewart – two non-pop-concert goers – have returned saying how impressed they were. Everybody is happy and relaxed and I get the feeling the mood is right again for the coming Test match, Newcastle forgotten and out of the system

Thursday 27 November

The news is better about John Emburey. He reported this morning that the trapped nerve pain has disappeared to such an extent he is looking for a game of golf in the afternoon. The final net session went very well and David Gower is also smiling again. He hit the ball right in the middle and emerged to say that he is ready for the Test now. Things are looking up. It is absolutely vital that we do not let the Australians back in.

The selection committee meeting was short, as could be expected after the Brisbane success, picking an unchanged 11. We decided not to name a 12th man as we knew 24 hours in advance of the match starting what our team would be. There had been some consideration to making Neil Foster 12th man for the way he has worked since Brisbane and his bowling has improved over the past fortnight. He has been as keen as anybody, but to make him 12th man would have meant demoting Gladstone Small, who had been in the Brisbane Test squad, which seemed silly because Gladstone had done nothing wrong.

All the reserves are special to us and to the outcome of the series. In the end we decided not to place one above the others as all five of them would be taking their turn anyway at carrying out the 12th man duties over the next five days.

There was something lacking at the team dinner this evening but I put that down to the fact that we were in a very large room instead of the smaller, more intimate one we had at Brisbane and the fact there was very little to be said except a few words about Geoff Lawson who was certain to play in the Australian side and leg spinner Peter Sleep from South Australia who had been called into the squad. We had seen him anyway.

Friday 28 November

If my face had registered misery over the toss in Brisbane, I wonder what it registered this morning when I called 'tails' and it came down the right way up. I had woken up thinking about the toss and how vital it was that we should win it, bat first and attempt to put the Australians under pressure while they were still reeling from the first Test hammering. My delight must have been obvious to everybody on the ground when I called correctly.

I don't have a special call. I'm not one for calling 'heads' or 'tails' all the time. I decided to call 'tails' today thinking of 'tails for Wales, and Perth is in the west of Australia'. All that mattered was that we won it and that Chris Broad and Bill Athey could strap on their pads. And what a superb response they made in putting on 223 before they were parted, allowing us to reach 272 for two by the end of the first day.

There was some considerable scrambling around for Micky Stewart to do before the game could start. Remembering the way that David Gower had been yorked by Bruce Reid in the state match against Western Australia, we had asked the local ground officials to extend the sight screen at the far end of the ground. Immediately behind it was some scaffolding holding a television camera crew and it had been draped with two large white pieces of material. But Micky spotted they were in the wrong position to cope with Reid's left-arm approach and he was still getting them re-arranged when the umpires walked out.

He had already put into practice another lesson learned from the Western Australia game when Ian Botham dropped two chances at slip, saying he had not seen the ball because it appeared out of a row of windows of a bar area next to the new grandstand the WACA ground now boasts. In order to get us used to the view Micky had given us slip catching practice out in the middle where we would actually be standing during the match, an eye for detail that might make all the difference.

The Australians had practised their early morning slip catching as normal on a spare part of the outfield. It might have made a difference if they had followed our example for it was at that end that Allan Border, at Botham's position of second slip, put down a Bill Athey edge against Chris Matthews in the eighth over preventing his side getting an early breakthrough. It was a strange lapse by Bill. He had been playing quietly when he suddenly opened up in a huge drive against the left-arm local bowler. The ball flew swiftly to Border's left and he did not appear to pick it up immediately.

It was possible that Bill was a little frustrated at the time, having been at the wicket for more than 30 minutes, yet scoring only three runs. Much of that was down to the fact that the Australian opening bowlers bowled so badly, Bill had very little scoring opportunities. Chris Matthews' first over to Chris Broad contained six balls down the offside – one a wide – and one down the leg side that did not require playing. Geoff Lawson was little better. He did beat Bill in his first over but the next was so wayward Bill was forced to play at only one delivery.

Whatever the reason Bill settled down to look very solid while Chris just grew and grew in authority. Our highest opening stand of the tour had been 16 scored in the game against New South Wales, but that was soon a thing of the past. There was only one other anxious moment when Bill played forward against Steve Waugh and the close-in fielders appealed for a catch behind. David Boon at first slip and Allan Border at second were very excited and stood their ground when umpire Dick French showed no response. It reached a point where Allan accused Bill of having touched the ball but Bill stood up for himself again. He told Australia's captain, 'If I had touched it I would admit it, but it came off my pad'. Again the television slow motion showed that the ball had missed the bat by almost an inch when it seamed back off the wicket and the deviation resulting in the catch appeal had been caused by the top of Bill's pad.

It was a good umpiring decision which allowed the pair to progress to 93 without loss at lunch and then 187 for nought at tea, each interval reached with Chris just short of a milestone, being 46 at lunch and 98 at tea. There was no sign of any nerves. In fact we were more nervous watching, wondering if it were all too good to be true. Padded up to go in at number three I know I was more tense for some reason when we had passed 100 without loss, than I had been when we were 30 or so. Graham Dilley and Ian Botham were even worse. They had been in the dressing room when the innings started and decided not to leave it and join the rest of us in the viewing area in case they broke the spell.

After sitting there for more than three hours with my pads on Allan Lamb took over the number three role for the last 20 minutes before tea to give me a rest. I was going to do the first hour again after tea and then have Allan stand guard for the final hour, all of us hoping that Chris and Bill would see out the day.

Bill did not, although he richly deserved to. We had all climbed to our feet as one man in the viewing area when Chris reached his maiden Test century after 249 minutes with 17 fours. We were preparing to do the same for Bill when he played over a full-length delivery from Reid and was bowled just four runs short. It was tragic but he had still played a part in establishing an England opening partnership record for the Perth ground.

By then Allan was in the number three spot again. Some 20 minutes after tea he had said he was keen to get going and would relieve me and I hoped that meant I wouldn't have to bat that day when Allan walked out. My relief did not last long. Within seven minutes Allan was on his way back and I was picking up my bat. I walked to the wicket, out through the tunnel from the new Perth dressing rooms into the open, rather like a soccer player, worried we may have a silly last hour that would wreck all the great work Chris and Bill had done. I was determined to stay there and told Chris not to worry about anything else except still being at the crease in the morning. I took more than half an hour to get off the mark but we both survived, including a spell looking after five overs of the second new ball.

Saturday 29 November

I woke up this morning thinking of terms of making 600 and then slipping the Australians in for half an hour. We didn't quite make the runs I wanted but it was still another magnificent day – after a few horror moments in the morning. I didn't see them apart from my own downfall.

The first aim for Chris and myself was simple. Stay around for at least an hour seeing off the new ball and then start to open up. I did not carry out my part of the bargain, adding only three more runs before getting out to a poor shot against left-arm pace-bowler Chris Matthews. He slanted a ball across me which looked safe enough to drive but I did not allow for the movement off the wicket so that I ended up reaching for it. I still got quite a lot of bat on it and thought I had escaped until Steve Waugh swooped in the gully. I felt sick and angry with myself. On my return to the dressing room I stayed around long enough to watch David Gower settle in with Chris, the pair of them looking good, before taking myself off to the nets to work off my frustration. The nets are away behind the terracing – and behind the scoreboard.

My mood was not helped when I heard a great roar not long after entering the nets. I knew from the noise that a wicket had fallen which meant that we were four down with our total not far beyond 300. It got worse. Another five minutes and another huge roar. Five down. Two out of Chris Broad, David Gower and Ian Botham had gone. I had no idea which two. I kept working in the nets waiting for further roars of disaster but nothing came apart from polite applause which signalled the odd boundary. Only then did I dare to venture back to the dressing room.

David Gower on his way to a hundred at Perth

The first sight that greeted me was Ian wearing a false plastic or rubber nose shaped in the form of a duck's bill! Then I spotted Chris and knew they were the two who had fallen during my absence at the nets. But David and Jack Richards were going well, the Australian field spread ever wider in an effort to contain them without succeeding. Their sixth-wicket 207-run partnership was almost worth the suffering caused by the agonies of the morning session. The toy duck's bill had been supplied that morning by Allan Lamb's wife Lyndsey following her husband's duck the previous evening. He had worn it in the dressing room first thing, and had no hesitation in handing it over to 'Beefy' Botham who sat wearing it throughout most of the Gower-Richards stand.

David was pure magic, rifling fours through the field with his superb timing and array of strokes, while Jack's innings was something special. This was only his second Test match, having made a duck in his first: it completely justified our action in picking him. He said afterwards that his best stroke was the push back past Reid which got him off the mark and brought him his first run in Test cricket. Jack seemed more pleased with that run than his maiden Test century.

It was proving a costly time for the management. Yesterday they had bought Chris champagne to celebrate his maiden Test century and they had to dig into the kitty again for Jack. There was another champagne bottle awaiting Chris when he returned to his hotel room from Ian Botham with a 'well done' message. That is a side of Ian that never gets mentions – simply because he never mentions it.

The loss of the four wickets in the morning had slowed us down but David and Jack put on 207 together for the sixth wicket in scoring their individual hundreds, and enabled me to declare with enough time to bowl seven overs at Australia. We took the wicket of David Boon who was caught in two minds in Graham Dilley's second over and paid the penalty, dragging the ball on to his wicket.

There was one further piece of encouragement for us tonight. I slipped John Emburey on for the last over and he made one turn sharply from out of the rough which Geoff Marsh was lucky not to touch. It wouldn't do the Australians any harm to sleep on that ball.

Sunday 30 November

Today was a let-down although we still finished with high hopes of making the Australians follow on for the second Test in succession. The turn we expected from the wicket just never happened. It was remarkable.

Small cracks were visable in the pitch when the Test had started and these had gradually widened under the hot sun. Today it was almost possible to slip the ends of my fingers down the cracks. There were also some rough patches left by the bowlers. But, in the case of the cracks and the rough, they were in the wrong places for John and Phil to exploit. The edges of the cracks stayed firm throughout the day and the pitch surface between was perfect.

David Gower congratulates Jack Richards on his maiden Test Century

Ian Botham captures the wicket of Geoff Marsh

Bill Athey holds the ball aloft after taking a brilliant catch to dismiss Dean Jones

We managed to get an early breakthrough when Chris Broad, standing backward of square, somehow hung on to a firm pull Marsh aimed against Beefy, but making progress during the rest of the day was a real grind.

Our catching helped us get through, following the example Chris had set. Bill Athey took another superb one at leg slip to get rid of Dean Jones, but Steve Waugh – who had come in as nightwatchman the previous evening – Allan Border, Greg Ritchie and Greg Matthews all held us up in their various ways.

For more than two hours Waugh showed us why, at the age of 21, Australia consider him one of their best young prospects and why they have stuck with him although he has made only one half century in his first 13 attempts in Test cricket. He made his second today. He plays with plenty of time against the faster bowlers.

There was a grim set about Border's face and shoulders when he walked out to bat and Ritchie played the spin bowlers particularly well, once hitting Phil over long on for six. Some people were apparently surprised when I split up the Edmonds-Emburey combination and brought Dilley back in the afternoon to have a go against Ritchie. All I can say is that they were not watching the confident way Ritchie played the slower bowlers.

Border was all grit and guts. Nothing would put him off his survival path. Not even Allan Lamb's antics at silly point. Allan had gone onto the field wearing the duck's nose tucked under his shirt. When Border walked to the crease, Allan got it out and tried to wave it under Border's nose more than once just for a lark. But Border was having none of it, refusing to look in Allan's direction all the time he was taking guard and weighing up the fielding positions.

We finished the day by taking one other splendid catch to have the sixth

Australian wicket down and I don't think the catcher has ever enjoyed one so much. Ian botham held it, a great diving effort to his left at second slip to get rid of Greg Matthews. Half an hour earlier I had taken the new ball in an attempt to disturb the Australian tail and Matthews had upset 'Beefy' by the way he had backed away and sliced him through the slip region – sometimes intentionally, often accidentally. At the start of Ian's fourth over with the new ball I had given him two slips. By the end of it we had four slips but still Matthews managed to find a way through, twice reaching the boundary. But when he tried to do exactly the same thing in Dilley's next over Ian dived to hold the catch. The sheer delight on his face had to be seen to be believed.

We did not help ourselves by our bowling. The faster bowlers were generally a little too short and did not keep the ball up around off stump as they had done in Brisbane. John Emburey could never manage the same control either, upset by the famous 'Fremantle Doctor' wind blowing strongly over the ground at times. Before the close he apologised to me and I can't ever remember him doing that before in all the years I have known him. He just wasn't happy with himself and, looking back on the day now, I suppose I would have been better off using Phil more.

Monday 1 December
For the second Test rest day in succession I found myself completely at ease with the world, contemplating another victory with the luxury of a lie-in. Although we had not performed as well as we might have done the previous day Allan Border was the captain with all the worries, Australia going into the fourth day of the game still needing another 84 runs with only four wickets left to avoid the follow-on.

I was determined to have a lazy day and I did. I did not go out for my usual round of golf with other players which is my normal rest-day routine because I just wanted to free my head of cricket for once, and be an ordinary human being. Instead I decided to visit Fremantle, still a hive of activity with the America's Cup centred there, although it was a 'lay' week allowing work and alterations to be carried out on the yachts in preparation for the last series of races before the field was reduced. Several of the players had already been entertained by the British *White Crusader* crew and found them confident of finishing in the top four after the first series of races which would be good enough to qualify for the later stages. We all believe our own schedule is hard enough but their workload was fantastic, starting early in the morning and finishing late at night, almost on the go the whole time. I had to admire them; I certainly didn't envy them! I must confess that I am not a sailor.

Fremantle has certainly been well spruced up for the occasion and to cope with the hordes of visitors, although many shop-owners were complaining that the number of tourists was well down on the estimated figure. At least I had no difficulty finding a nice place for lunch. I spent a quiet evening over a few drinks before going early to bed. A nice relaxing day. I wish there were more of them on this tour.

Tuesday 2 December

This has been Australia's day – just. I suppose there is some consolation in the fact that it is the first time in nine Test playing days that they have managed to get the better of things, and in the fact that we can't lose this match which means that Australia's second best chance of winning a Test has gone.

There would have been a chance of us losing it tomorrow if I had taken all the advice that has been handed me this evening about declaring earlier. I have been surprised by the number of people who have asked why I didn't declare to give England 30 or 40 minutes bowling at Australia a second time in the hope of taking a wicket or two. To have done that would have meant declaring when we were about 340 ahead and then set attacking fields to the new ball on a wicket that was still playing well and offering little assistance to any bowler. Perhaps we might have taken one wicket, possibly two. On the other hand they might have scored 30 or 40 runs with close-in fielders on a very fast outfield where the ball generally went to the boundary once it got through. Now, Australia entering the last day tomorrow needing 300 to win with all wickets intact would have been a very tempting proposition for them and I decided I could not take that risk. I would have looked an idiot of a captain if I should lose when my batsmen have given me 592 runs in the first innings. I would never have been able to look any of them in the eye again. No, I think I did the right thing by batting until the close of play giving us a 390 lead.

The first part of the day was definitely Allan Border's as he reached his 20th Test century, and made sure that Australia did not have to follow on. It was a magnificent effort spread over 372 minutes. What a plucky little fighter he is. I had to admire him. I thought he also took some extraordinary risks as well. I still had high hopes of making them bat again when we got rid of Tim Zoehrer, Geoff Lawson and Chris Matthews, chipping away slowly. When Bruce Reid walked out to join his captain, Australia were eight runs away from being safe and we were in with a shout.

Border had encouraged us during his partnership with Matthews when he seemed to have no worries about exposing his number 10 batsman to five balls an over. I spread the field to give Border one at the start of an over and he took it, leaving us to have a go at his partner. Perhaps he did not think at that stage the follow-on could be saved despite his own mammoth efforts. When Reid joined him, Border again exposed his last man for the first couple of overs before taking charge of the last-wicket partnership, signalling safety when cutting John Emburey to the boundary.

The Plan 'A' scheme enforcing the follow-on had failed. It was time to fall back on Plan 'B' for our second victory effort. That was chasing quick runs in order to get Australia in again before the close but giving them no scent of victory. Border foiled us there as well.

He closed us down well with his defensive fields using the controlled left-arm medium pace of Reid and the occasional medium pace of Waugh to make batting difficult as each bowler found a good line and length.

I thought we had a chance of doubling our 191 first-innings lead half an hour before the scheduled close when David Gower started hitting the ball brilliantly again after we had lost our first three wickets for 50 runs. I let him have his head when we batted together. Towards the end of the partnership I was beginning to strike out myself with 50 runs behind me but was forced to change my ideas when David edged behind a drive aimed against Waugh. I could see us collapsing badly if we became too ambitious.

The captain in action

It was disappointing having the brake put on us. It was altogether a frustrating day. But I live in hope something will happen to those cracks tomorrow when I shall be able to attack with fielders around the bat not worrying about the boundaries.

Wednesday 3 December

The edges of the cracks refused to crumble. Another day of frustration, especially since it was one that had started so promisingly when David Boon's bat was drawn to the very first ball of the day from Graham Dilley and he edged a perfect outswinger to second slip. It was not until mid-afternoon that we were able to manage another wicket, although John Emburey was bowling near to his Brisbane standard.

I tried every permutation I could think of in an effort to disturb Geoff Marsh and Dean Jones during their 126-run second-wicket partnership but notning could disturb them. In the end it needed a startling run-out from Chris Broad to separate them and re-awaken our interest. What a magnificent game he is having.

Jones had tried one or two risky runs before in his 69-run innings, playing as if this were a one-day match and Australia were chasing a victory instead of playing out time. He has a habit of pushing at the ball and then setting off for a swift single that startled Marsh more than once. This time he chanced his arm once too often when he drove DeFreitas to mid-off and hared down the track. He was only half way down when Chris swooped and hurled down the wicket at the bowler's end although he had little more than one stump to aim at from his angle. It was close but Jones was beaten by a foot.

That rekindled our hopes. They were raised again when Marsh fell leg before offering no stroke against Emburey. And once more when Allan Border was taken off bat and pad at short leg two balls after tea. Knowing how much the Australians rely on Border, I thought they might then crack if we could pressurise them into further errors. Greg Ritchie and Greg Matthews were having none of it.

Looking back on their partnership now, some four hours later as I write these notes, I must say they did a good job although they annoyed us at the time by their time-wasting tactics, trying to cut down the number of overs before the last hour started. Both of them were forever holding up play, 'gardening' on the pitch which is always frustrating for a spin bowler. Like any other bowler they like to get into a rhythm and nothing is more annoying than being forced to wait at the start of their run, however short it may be.

The tension was building up a little when both Ritchie and Matthews objected to the shadow caused by Bill Athey standing at short leg. There was never a problem, with Bill crouching low to make sure his shadow did not spread across the wicket when the ball was delivered, but Ritchie made a big song and dance about it on one occasion, holding up play by protesting to the umpires. The tension was broken by Graham Dilley who was fielding on the boundary. He shouted across, 'It's a good job 'Gatt' isn't fielding there. With his shadow, we would all be off for bad light'. I couldn't understand what he was getting at!

With ten of the last 20 overs to go I agreed to call off the hunt, Australia having lost just four wickets at that stage. We'd had a good go. The soundness of the wicket had defeated us even though the cracks in the pitch were now so wide it was possible to get almost half my hand down them.

It was deeply disappointing considering the way we had batted in the first innings. Performances like the ones from Chris, David and Jack deserved a better ending than a drawn game. In addition to my disappointment I had another worry – Ian Botham.

I'd brought Ian back into the attack soon after lunch in the hope of disturbing Marsh and Jones. During his second over he made a great effort to surprise Jones by trying to obtain a little extra bounce out of the pitch, bowling him a shortish ball. It didn't work. Jones simply pulled him for four. Even worse was the pull Ian suffered – in the rib area on his left side, forcing him to wince in agony. He attempted to bowl the next ball but as soon as he stretched just before delivery, the pain was so severe he pulled up immediately, dropped the ball and walked off, telling me he just could not carry on. For Ian to do that in the middle of a Test match I knew it must be serious.

My fears were confirmed when I returned to the dressing room at the end of the match and Laurie Brown told me he had certainly strained a rib muscle, possibly torn it slightly. It is a fairly common injury among fast bowlers. I imagine every county must suffer one per season. It is also extremely unpleasant, the next worse injury to suffering a groin strain.

Ian himself told me it was the most painful injury he had suffered in cricket – and he has put up with a lot, insisting on playing with injuries that would have forced many others to cry off. I fear he will be out of the next Test in Adelaide, possibly the next one in Melbourne, too. It put a damper on all proceedings.

SECOND TEST MATCH

WACA Ground, Perth, November 28, 29, 30, December 2, 3

ENGLAND		Runs	Mins	Balls	4s		Runs	Mins	Balls	4s
B.C. Broad	c Zoehrer b Reid	162	435	303	25	lbw b Waugh	16	61	49	2
C.W.J. Athey	b Reid	96	285	253	11	c Border b Reid	6	12	11	1
A.J. Lamb	c Zoehrer b Reid	0	6	5	—	(4) lbw b Reid	2	4	6	—
*M.W. Gatting	c Waugh b Matthews, C.	14	83	60	2	(3) b Waugh	70	189	129	8
D.I. Gower	c Waugh b Matthews, G.	136	277	179	19	c Zoehrer b Waugh	48	71	56	7
I.T. Botham	c Border b Reid	0	6	5	—	c Matthews, G. b Reid	6	27	23	—
†C.J. Richards	c Waugh b Matthews, C.	133	241	209	16	c Lawson b Waugh	15	50	38	1
P.A.J. DeFreitas	lbw b Matthews, C.	11	19	15	1	b Waugh	15	11	11	3
J.E. Emburey	not out	5	6	7	—	not out	4	5	3	—
P.H. Edmonds	did not bat									
G.R. Dilley	did not bat									
Extras	(b4, lb15, w3, nb13)	35				(b4, lb9, nb4)	17			
	(8 wkts dec)	592				(8 wkts dec)	199			

Fall: 223, 227, 275, 333, 339, 546, 585, 592.

Fall: 8, 47, 50, 123, 140, 172, 190, 199.

Bowling: Lawson 41-8-126-0, Matthews, C. 29.1-4-112-3, Reid 40-8-115-4, Waugh 24-4-90-0, Matthews, G. 34-3-124-1, Border 2-0-6-0.

Reid 21-3-58-3, Lawson 9-1-44-0, Waugh 21.3-4-69-5, Matthews, C. 2-0-15-0.

AUSTRALIA

		Runs	Mins	Balls	4s			Runs	Mins	Balls	4s
G.R. Marsh	c Broad b Botham	15	81	65	—	(2) lbw b Emburey		49	202	148	7
D.C. Boon	b Dilley	2	6	3	—	(1) c Botham b Dilley		0	1	1	—
S.R. Waugh	c Botham b Emburey	71	143	109	4*						
D.M. Jones	c Athey b Edmonds	27	89	88	2	(3) run out (Broad)		69	168	157	8
*A.R. Border	c Richards b Dilley	125	372	284	17	(4) c Lamb b Edmonds		16	71	66	3
G.M. Ritchie	c Botham b Edmonds	33	85	65	6	(5) not out		24	134	136	3
G.R.J. Matthews	c Botham b Dilley	45	94	79	8	(6) not out		14	95	85	1
†T.J. Zoehrer	lbw b Dilley	29	61	55	5						
G.F. Lawson	b DeFreitas	13	32	27	—						
C.D. Matthews	c Broad b Emburey	10	44	40	1						
B.A. Reid	not out	2	24	10	—						
Extras	(b9, lb9, nb11)	29				(b9, lb6, nb10)		25			
		401	*Plus 1 six				(4 wkts)	197			

Fall: 4, 64, 114, 128, 198, 279, 334, 360, 385, 401.

Bowling: Botham 22-4-72-1, Dilley 24.4-4-79-4,
Emburey 43-9-110-2, DeFreitas 24-4-67-1,
Edmonds 21-4-55-2.

0, 126, 142, 152.
Dilley 15-1-53-1, Botham 7.2-4-13-0,
DeFreitas 13.4-2-47-0, Emburey 28-11-41-1,
Edmonds 27-13-25-1, .Gatting 5-3-3-0,
Lamb 1-1-0-0.

Toss won by England
Man of the Match: B.C. Broad

Umpires: R.A. French & P.J. McConnell

MATCH DRAWN

Stalemate at Adelaide

Thursday 4 December

Another of those wasted days on tour, another change in time zone for the body to adjust to, moving on to Melbourne for the first time and the match against Victoria at the weekend which threatens to be a hard one. They are currently on top of the Sheffield Shield competition and favourites to win the title with their side boasting half a dozen Test players.

Our concern was over the fitness of Ian Botham, hoping that a night's rest would have eased the pain and given us some clue as to how long we might be without him. The news is not good. Any movement that forced him to bend forward or sideways hurt him and even coughing was painful. It was decided to get him to a specialist as soon as possible to confirm Laurie's assessment of the damage.

Tonight I repaid a debt to an old friend, Peter Spencer. He was cricket coach at New South Wales when I played grade cricket in Balmain and I stayed at his house. He is now looking after the Kanga cricket scheme on behalf of the Australian Cricket Board and is based in Melbourne. Kanga is a form of cricket played in schools to introduce children of around eight or nine to the game. It is played with plastic bats and stumps and with a soft ball so that young girls and boys can take up the sport without any thought of getting hurt. It is proving successful in countering forms of sport in schools threatening to attract youngsters away from cricket.

Peter asked me if I would attend a dinner to raise funds for the family of Doug Rumble, a Melbourne cricketer who along with his wife had tragically died in a skiing accident. It was a last-minute invitation but I'm glad I went. The hosts were very appreciative. I had difficulty falling asleep when I got back to the hotel with my body still on Perth time.

Friday 5 December

We had one piece of good news today – the specialist confirmed that there is a slight tear of the muscle in Ian's ribs. Laurie's diagnosis had been spot on. A badly torn muscle might have put Ian out for the rest of the series but there was a chance now he might make the Adelaide Test if only as a batsman.

The players who had missed out at Perth had a work-out this morning but I decided along with Micky that the rest could have a free day. We were all feeling a little drained. Even the media people travelling around with us confessed that the majority had been so tired they slept 10 hours without waking.

Finished the day with Peter Spencer again but this was far from formal. He invited me along to a barbecue at his home with a few other friends, a most relaxing evening over a steak and a beer or two, finished off with a couple of glasses of port. Back at the hotel I phoned my wife Elaine around one in the morning, knowing she would be at home – it was about 2pm in London. Working out the right time to phone home without disturbing people in the middle of the night is always a problem when you are constantly adjusting watches.

Saturday 6 December

Disaster, absolute disaster. And I was the cause of it. Oversleeping so that I missed the toss of the coin and even the start of the four-day game against Victoria which was starting half and hour earlier than usual each day to accommodate our swift departure for Adelaide on the final day. It was a very black mark for the captain. It was stupid, silly, unprofessional. All of those things. It was also very much out of character. And so easily done.

The first I was aware of the disaster was a hard pummelling on my hotel room door. I opened it to find Chris Broad standing there looking most concerned. He told me it was ten minutes past ten. I just had no idea of the time. He had been sent back from the ground to find me when I failed to show up. It was only then that I realised my plight. There was just time for a quick shower, a dash to the ground, quick change and rush on to the field some 20 minutes after the match had started with David Gower in command, vice captain John Emburey having been given the match off.

My unfortunate sleep-in had been caused by a series of accidents and misunderstandings. When speaking to my wife during the early hours of the morning I had stretched out on top of the bedclothes, still almost fully dressed. I had put the phone back on its modern cradle, but not quite properly. It had not connected. Then I had obviously fallen asleep straight away, having had difficulty in getting to sleep the previous evening. With the phone off the hook, it gave out an engaged tone when Micky Stewart had tried to phone me in the morning when I wasn't spotted in the lobby at the time we were all due to leave. It was assumed, quite naturally, that I was up speaking on the telephone. To make the situation slightly more difficult, we were travelling to and from the ground in a series of cars and not by coach where my absence would have been spotted in a routine check. It was not until I failed to show for the warm-up practice before the start of the game that I was really missed and the management became concerned. The previous day Allan Lamb had been forced to miss the nets because of a stomach bug. He still wasn't well and it was thought I might be ill as well. That is when Chris was sent back to fetch me. My phone was still engaged when he tried my room which led to the hard banging on the door.

It was very embarrassing for all concerned, especially me. I felt sorry for Micky and Peter Lush because it made them look a little silly turning up at the ground without a captain. I had time for just a quick apology with no explanations when I arrived at the ground. I was needed swiftly on the field because I was wanted for bowling with Victoria having batted first and with us fielding only Neil Foster and Gladstone Small of the faster men.

That led to ridiculous charges that Peter was involved in an attempted cover-up when he was finaly able to give the media an explanation after lunchtime. One story had already been sent out regarding my absence suggesting I was 'indisposed'. That was the first thought anyway. It was only at lunch when Peter and Micky tackled me that I had the first chance to explain and also apologise to the team as a whole for putting unnecessary pressure on them. Rightly Peter had a go at me, for it was something that should not have happened. Fortunately, most people found it more amusing than serious. There was certainly no insult intended to anybody. It was probably doubly unfortunate that the Victoria state game was being staged as the 'Sir Robert Menzies Memorial Match' which meant there were extra officials and dignitaries there on the opening morning.

By lunchtime I was feeling a little better about it. The Melbourne pitch was not a good one, helping swing and seam bowling and the Victorian batsmen made a hash of playing it. I managed to nip in with a couple of wickets before lunch and another two after the break. I emerged from the innings with four for 31 aided by Neil Foster taking three catches at long leg off hooks and pulls. I felt for Neil and Gladstone Small. Both had bowled better than I had done and deserved greater success than mine. By the close we had moved 27 runs ahead at 128 for six, the one disappointment being James Whitaker's duck batting at number three. We had sent him in early to give him the chance of playing a long innings.

Sunday 7 December
My sleep-in and not the actual cricket was still the main topic of conversation today. I was surprised by the anger in some reports in English newspapers written by cricket writers, including one or two who frequently arrive late in the press box, particularly at home Test matches. There were even dark suggestions reading between the lines of some reports that there was something more sinister behind my sleep-in, in the way Fleet Street has of refusing to accept explanations. I was even more annoyed to hear that one paper had quoted a 'senior player' as saying 'Gatting should not be allowed to get away with it. If it had been Ian Botham, it would have been front page news.'

I didn't get away with anything. I was rightly rebuked by the management who took into account my good track record. Ian Botham would not have been treated any differently if it had happened to him. At least by us. If Fleet Street had chosen to blow it up out of all proportion because of his name, there is nothing we could have done about it. If I had wanted to get away with anything, the way out was to have pretended I had a stomach upset and nothing would have been said. But I was late, I was guilty and I was prepared to face the consequences.

It was a pity this was overshadowing the cricket. Out in the middle Bruce French, Allan Lamb – recovered from his stomach upset – and Neil Foster all combined to give us a 162-run lead before rain interrupted the rest of the day and prevented us making a serious assault on Victoria's second innings.

The whole day ended in a touch of farce when the umpires made a third attempt to get play going although it was pouring with rain. I just couldn't believe they were serious. My sweater was wet just walking down the pavilion steps to the outfield. I know they are used to playing in bad conditions in local grade cricket in attempts to get matches finished but this was a game involving an international side and I was reluctant to risk injury to my players on a very wet outfield with the Third Test just around the corner. Allan Lamb seemed to make up the minds of the umpires that the conditions were too bad. He borrowed an umbrella a spectator had been sheltering under on the boundary edge and walked with it to his fielding position. The umpires took one look at him and abandoned play for the day! It was a smart move by Allan.

Monday 8 December

With Ian Botham definitely out of consideration for the Adelaide Test as a bowler we were all encouraged today by a superb bowling performance from Gladstone Small who was finally getting the luck he deserved.

He put us in line for our second victory over a state side by finishing the day with five for 70 off 35 overs although the wicket had dried out and the batting was easier. He kept the ball pitched up, bowled in the channel, as Micky calls it, around off stump and beat the batsmen with both his movement off the wicket and swing. Nobody took any liberties with him, not even Test batsmen Paul Hibbert and Simon O'Donnell who provided Victoria's main resistance with half centuries. I went to bed happy – and early – that Gladstone was ready for the Adelaide Test if we were to need him.

Tuesday 9 December

Things are really looking up. A very satisfying victory and two more encouraging performances from Neil Foster and James Whitaker. They paved the way to our five-wicket win after we had been left to score 184 in a minimum of 46 overs.

Neil's contribution was in knocking over the Victoria tail in the morning with a three-wicket burst at the cost of 28 runs in ten overs. He was producing some very good wicket-taking deliveries but my worry over him was his inclination to stray either side of the wicket that could prove very costly on a good batting pitch. Gladstone Small was the tighter bowler.

Micky and I had been discussing the make-up of the Third Test side if Ian was ruled out completely, and we were both of the opinion it would be better to play an extra batsman in the Adelaide conditions. That pointed to James, but he desperately needed runs today after his first-innings duck before we could risk him. He provided them.

We again sent him in at number three to give him the opportunity and he emerged with 48 runs out of a 74-run stand with Wilf Slack and provided the basis for our victory rush later in the innings. He struck the ball confidently, finding the boundary seven times before being caught at slip attempting to sweep Victoria's captain and left-arm spinner Ray Bright who had been called into Australia's Test squad the previous day. James played particularly well against fast bowler Merv Hughes who had also been recalled for the Adelaide Test, with Australia dropping Geoff Lawson and Chris Matthews after their wayward performances in Perth.

We did have one new area of concern in addition to Ian when we made our dash from the ground to catch the evening flight to Adelaide. Bruce French had been struck in the ribs by Hughes during his innings two days previously which had prevented him keeping wicket. Fortunately we had played Jack Richards in the match as a batsman so he was able to take over.

Bruce was still feeling the injury although an x-ray had shown no sign of a break. We needed him fit to act as cover for Jack in Adelaide but he wasn't too confident he would be able to provide that cover.

My sleep-in had not been forgotten either. As we took off this evening the stewardess at the rear of the plane went through the usual safety check on the aircraft and then added, 'May I ask all passengers to converse very quietly during the rest of the flight as I understand the England captain is trying to get to sleep!' One of the pressmen had put her up to it.

England XI v Victoria (Sir Robert Menzies Memorial Match)
Played at Melbourne, Dec 6, 7, 8, 9.

Victoria 101 and 345 (P.A. Hibbert 91, S.P. O'Donnell 77
G.C. Small 5 for 81)
England XI 263 (C.W.J. Athey 58, B.N. French 58 and 184 for 5)

England XI won by 5 wickets.

Wednesday 10 December

Ian was dominating all our thoughts at this moment and there was a sign of slight improvement today. He had been swimming daily for the last four days as well as having treatment twice a day from Laurie. He was desperately keen to play and I could see a danger of Ian declaring himself fit in his keenness yet not really being up to performing properly as a batsman. We had already ruled out any chance of him bowling. I wanted him in the side if at all possible because the Australians were obviously inhibited by him.

My other problem was what to do with Ian in the field if he did play as a batsman. The pain he felt was in bending and I could not risk him at first slip. It was going to be a delicate decision. I slept on it.

Thursday 11 December

I did not have to worry when Ian came down to the ground this morning to have a try-out as a batsman. It lasted just one ball. A slow, underarm throw from Micky on the outfield. That was all Ian needed to know he couldn't make it. He threw away his bat and walked sadly back to the dressing room.

We had two alternatives. We could play James Whitaker as a batsman or use Ian's place to bring in an extra seam bowler, probably Gladstone Small. Micky and I looked at the pitch along with John Emburey and David Gower and it appeared a beauty, a pitch made for runs. There was nothing in it to suggest any help for the faster bowlers and we opted for James making his Test début. To confirm our feelings we asked Gladstone Small for his opinion of the wicket. He had played on the Adelaide Oval the previous winter for South Australia and knew the conditions well. He agreed he would probably get little or nothing out of it.

That settled the issue as we named a straight 11 again tonight with James for Ian the only change. It was a defensive move but we felt we needed to make sure we held the Australians in this particular match especially with Ian missing. We had to be able to match whatever runs they made particularly if I should lose the toss and they batted first.

I did not think a third seam bowler would get much bowling. In the match against South Australia over a month earlier, Phil Edmonds and John Emburey had done 80 per cent of the bowling. They were going to do so again over the next five days once the shine was off the ball. I thought that if we were going to be without Ian for a game, this was the best place, a game where he would be lucky to bowl more than ten overs in an innings even if fully fit. It was also up to the Australians to make a move as they were the side trailing by one Test. I was rather surprised they went into the game with a similar line-up to ours with Merv Hughes and Bruce Reid the only fast bowlers supported by Steve Waugh's medium pace. I felt confident we could at least hold them, leaving us to go into the last two Tests on result wickets in a very healthy position.

Friday 12 December
I lost the toss and feared that Australia would do to us what we did to them on the first day in Perth. To make things even worse, neither Graham Dilley nor Phillip DeFreitas bowled well with the new ball which helped Australia get a start. Yet, tonight, I'm more than content. We had limited Australia to 207 for two in a full day's play and that was a marvellous effort. John and Phil were our bowling heroes.

The waste of the new ball was disappointing and I could not put all the blame on the bowlers. Picca Dilley just couldn't get the ball in the right spot while Daffy DeFreitas was no-balled several times for overstepping. Neither had bowled since the Perth Test, and I made a mental note as they struggled to make sure in future that both be made to bowl off full runs in net sessions – or elsewhere – to get their rhythm back before playing in another Test. I was reminded of an incident with Middlesex some years ago when we decided not to play Wayne Daniel and Vincent van der Bijl against Cambridge University to save them for a vital championship game that followed. Although they had been without cricket for only three days, they found their rhythm had gone when it came to the morning of the championship match and their bowling suffered.

Daffy bowled very well, despite no-ball problems

What was particularly annoying about DeFreitas' early spell was that he bowled a number of very good deliveries. Twice he caught David Boon plumb in front, so plumb that the umpires would have been forced to give him out leg before. Unfortunately both were against no-balls. The Tasmanian survived and after only 12 overs the Australians had put 44 runs on the board. I was quickly forced to turn to John and Phil to establish some sort of control and they did so for the rest of the day.

It was a good battle of wits between bat and ball. My fields were not ambitious but it was up to the Australian batsmen to make the running with everything in their favour. They never managed to break loose. We were undoubtedly helped by the fact that Boon was not in the best of form. Once he had survived the new ball – for the first time in the series – he took great care to make his innings count.

We had one stroke of luck when Geoff Marsh went to sweep Phil after more than three hours at the crease scoring his 43 only to be bowled off his pad and elbow. The incoming Dean Jones was also in trouble making headway against the slow bowlers and even Allan Border was sedate when taking over from Boon whose 103 had taken him just over five hours. I was very happy with our position in limiting Australia but with only two wickets down I thought they were well prepared to get cracking on the second day.

Saturday 13 December

Again the day finishing slightly in our favour although Australia managed to score 514 for the loss of five wickets before Border declared. Yet he must have been disappointed with that score. He must have been hoping for something nearer

Steve Waugh, 79 not out in the first innings

600. It was not until the final 40 minutes of their innings when Greg Matthews and Steve Waugh, particularly the latter, started taking chances that they began to score at the pace they should have been doing some three hours earlier.

Once again we had controlled the first four hours of the day by accurate bowling so that Jones, Border and Greg Ritchie never plundered the runs they wanted to. The first two were just starting to get on top when both were out, somewhat unluckily.

Border was the first to go when he played forward defensively to Phil only for the thin nick to get tangled up in his body giving Jack Richards the chance to scuttle around the leg side and hold a catch in front of the wicket. Jones was only seven runs short of his century when he hooked at Graham Dilley and got the thinnest of edges to give a catch behind.

Ritchie was trying to get a move on when he drove a catch to mid-on leaving Waugh to take the initiative for the Australians, while Matthews struggled for more than an hour reaching double figures. He held up Australia as much as our slow bowlers.

I was still a little surprised when Border declared, leaving us to face the final 30 minutes of the day. We needed to score 315 to save the follow-on and I saw no reason why we should not do that. I think I would have batted on into the third day and made sure of 600 on the board. Our danger period was the last 30 minutes of the day but Chris Broad and Bill Athey negotiated them so well they scored 29, Chris taking advantage of the attacking field to hit out positively.

Century-maker Chris Broad hits out . . .

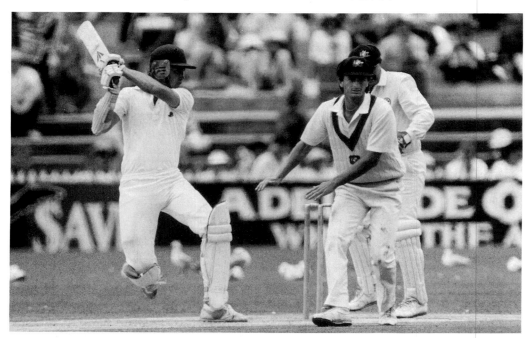

Sunday 14 December

I left the ground disappointed this evening although I had scored a century, Chris Broad had scored another and we saved the follow-on with only three wickets down. We should never have lost more than two but ended up giving away five which I felt put the Australians right back in the hunt with a victory chance.

Border had hoped to unsettle us by using the leg spin of Peter Sleep on his home ground but the South Australian wrist spinner was never more threatening than tidy even if he did take the only wicket before lunch when Bill Athey chopped on with the score showing 112. Then it was time for my entrance.

I had not set any specific targets at the start of the day as far as runs were concerned but had made it clear that I would have liked us to have batted for two days. I had thought this should give us a sizeable first innings lead and we could have Australia in trouble on the final day.

Both Chris and I found scoring relatively easy. Chris found it a tougher mental battle than at Perth because he was up against more spin this time and he is the first to admit that spinners do bother him. He did have one or two alarms against Sleep but generally he coped with it well.

I am fortunate that I don't have that trouble. I grew up as a kid playing against a good leg spinner and I have generally found it possible to read them through the air once I have had a chance to study them. Sleep did not offer much in the way of variation, bowling mostly leg breaks with the occasional top spinner. I don't think he attempted to serve me up a googly. Strangely, I was never really confident

. . . my own score was exactly 100 . . .

. . . but in the second innings I was bowled out for a duck by Greg Matthews

when I came up against off spinners during my first few years in county cricket. I could play them off my legs when they strayed in line or drive them through the extra-cover area, but found other scoring strokes difficult to execute. I never dreamed of smashing them through the wide mid-wicket or mid-on area until I studied Keith Fletcher closely during the 1981–82 tour of India. Even then it took me another season and endless net sessions with Middlesex coach Don Bennett before I felt confident to play it out in the middle. These days I find it a rewarding stroke against off spinners.

I managed to hit Greg Matthews through there more than once during my first 50 runs, until Border thought it wiser to take his off spinner out of the attack. Chris Broad went on to reach his century in 259 minutes just before tea, by which time our partnership had grown to 108.

During the break I suggested to Chris that we should take it steady for the first hour after tea and then start looking for runs more quickly. I hoped we might both be there at the close. We saw the hour out but then things started to go wrong. Chris was the first to go, when our second-wicket stand had put on 161 in 45 overs, pulling Waugh to mid-wicket, Marsh taking a good catch low down by his ankles with the ball having come off the middle of Chris's bat.

I was the next. I reached my century in three hours driving Sleep straight for four, only to get out next ball caught at mid-wicket pulling. The ball deserved to be hit although it turned a little more than I expected, with the result I caught it higher on the bat than I wanted. Anyway, it looked a horrible stroke when I watched the television replay in the dressing room.

That was not the end of it. I commented to Allan Lamb and David Gower that we could not afford to lose another wicket before the close but they both got out. Lamb got into trouble against Hughes and the new ball, holing out to mid-off when he was starting to hit out and David was leg before to Reid, having already escaped one chance.

I had already asked John Emburey to go in as nightwatchman when Lamb was out in order to protect James Whitaker from an awkward début, but I had no alternative but to put James in to face the last three overs when Gower was out, four wickets having gone down for 68 runs. John did his job so well that James faced only one ball this evening.

It was all so frustrating because I thought we had given Allan Border a glimmer of hope by our action. A collapse in the morning would leave then 100-plus ahead, plenty of time to build a substantial lead and have us grovelling on the final day. The wicket was beginning to help the spinners.

Monday 15 December

John Emburey removed all our worries today. Instead of us being under pressure, we finished back in with another chance when he snatched three Australian wickets before the close.

John did a superb nightwatchman's job, turning it into a day-time occupation as well, putting in more than two hours overtime with the bat. I was sorry James

Whitaker did not manage to hang around longer at the start of the day. I've been excited by his strokeplay in the nets but it is difficult to keep on top of your form playing an innings about once a week as he has been doing.

Jack Richards played another good innings, helping John take the score from 361 for six to 422 for seven. By the time the innings finished in mid-afternoon on the fourth day with John having made 49 in almost three hours, we were only 59 runs behind. Perhaps the feature of the performance was John's 'collapsing' sweep stroke which ends up with him sprawled all over the wicket. He gets his left foot so far down the pitch that he overbalances in making contact with the ball. I've seen it countless times in England but this was Australia's first view of it – much to the amusement of Channel 9 who replayed it time and again.

John Emburey plays his revolutionary sweep shot

I was even entertaining thoughts this evening that we might sneak a win. In the final three hours today Graham Dilley bowled a really fast new-ball spell to dismiss Dean Jones, and Phillip DeFreitas finally got David Boon leg before with a legitimate delivery to leave the Australians on eight for two.

Daffy's strike was first, coming in his second over, leaving Boon with a duck to follow his first-innings century. He was quickly presented with the duck's nose to wear that evening. Jones was surprised by a great ball from Dilley that took off from just short of a length and he had no chance of getting his bat out of the way as he protected his face. It was Dilley's fastest spell of the tour and the batsmen were having great difficulty coping with him and the bounce he was getting, although the wicket was now four days old. When Jones was out Australia had made only eight runs from the first 11 overs.

My hopes were kindled further when Phil tempted Geoff Marsh into driving a simple return catch so that by the end of the day Australia were 82 for three, 141 runs on. If we could separate Allan Border and Greg Ritchie early in the morning we might even be in with a shout. At least we should not lose now. There was alwlays a chance Border would set up a tempting target, too, in an effort to win the match for Australia.

Tuesday 16 December

My hopes and, I suppose, those of Allan Border's that each might somehow strangle a victory out of the game, disappeared today when rain washed out half the morning session. It became clear at lunch-time that the game was not going to get anywhere. By then Australia were 190 ahead without having lost another wicket – not enough for Allan to declare – and we were never going to be bowled out by the time the declaration came.

The game just drifted as Allan collected his 21st Test century which occupied almost five hours. I suppose our only triumph of the day was to shackle Greg Ritchie so that even at the end of his 207-minute stay he had still not reached 50 when the tea-time declaration was made. He looked more out of touch the longer he spent at the crease.

We went out again 260 behind, with 90 minutes left before the match was going to be called off. Long enough for Bill Athey to get out and for me to be dismissed first ball. Like Boon, I had followed a first-innings century with a duck and he lost no time in handing over the duck's nose for me to have my turn with it!

Neither Bill nor myself were switched on enough to play the type of innings needed to see out time. We both found it difficult to concentrate and paid the penalty. It was, I suppose, unprofessional.

This evening I have been surprised by the number of cricket writers – both English and Australian – who said they found the whole Test match boring and blamed the wicket for being too good. I admit it wasn't a particularly sparkling game, although we had done our best to liven it up on the third day when scoring 320 runs off 93 overs. Not bad for a side that was supposed to be fighting to save the game. I'd call that pretty enterprising and entertaining. There was also some very good cricket played for the purists, especially in the way we managed to contain the Australian batsmen over the first two days when they were hoping to score quickly. By the fourth evening a victory for either side was still possible, which doesn't suggest a bore. I suppose most people had written the game off as a draw before a ball had been bowled and that conditions their minds before the start.

Certainly Les Burdett's pitch could not be blamed. It offered an increasing amount of turn from the third day onwards, which in my opinion makes it a good Test pitch. And Graham Dilley showed on the fourth afternoon that there was still some life in it for a faster bowler who was prepared to bend his back.

I was happy enough with it and with our situation. Our batting was now looking extrmely solid, each first innings topping 450 runs thanks to the platform the openers had been able to put down. Allan Border commented at this evening's press conference that as long as we continued to make 450 runs every time we batted then there was no way the Australians would be able to get back into the series, needing to win both the final Test matches. I also held high hopes for the two remaining Tests because I fancied our attack against the Australian batsmen on pitches offering more help than usual – as Melbourne and Sydney threatened to do.

Looking back on the 15 days of Test cricket so far I calculated that we had had the better of 13 of those days and Allan was generous enough to say tonight that we deserved to be in the position we are because we had played the better cricket throughout.

THIRD TEST MATCH

Adelaide Oval, December 12, 13, 14, 15, 16

AUSTRALIA		Runs	Mins	Balls	4s		Runs	Mins	Balls	4s
G.R. Marsh	b Edmonds	43	193	137	5	(2) c & b Edmonds	41	144	95	5
D.C. Boon	c Whitaker b Emburey	103	302	274	14	(1) lbw b DeFreitas	0	16	11	—
D.M. Jones	c Richards b Dilley	93	282	221	9	c Lamb b Dilley	2	30	21	—
*A.R.Border	c Richards b Edmonds	70	150	129	7*	not out	100	303	253	11
G.M. Ritchie	c Broad b DeFreitas	36	85	56	3	not out	46	207	162	2
G.R.J. Matthews	not out	73	180	120	4**					
S.R. Waugh	not out	79	118	106	10					
P.R. Sleep	did not bat									
†G.C.Dyer	did not bat									
M.G. Hughes	did not bat									
B.A. Reid	did not bat									
Extras	(lb2, nb15)	17				(b3, lb7, nb2)	12			
	(5 wkts dec)	514				(3 wkts dec)	201			

*Plus 1 five
**Plus 1 six 1, 8, 77.

Fall: 113, 185, 311, 333, 368.
Bowling: Dilley 32-3-111-1, DeFreitas 32-4-128-1, Emburey 46-11-117-1, Edmonds 52-14-134-2, Gatting 9-1-22-0.

Dilley 21-8-38-0, DeFreitas 16-5-36-1, Emburey 22-6-50-0, Edmonds 29-7-63-1, Gatting 2-1-4-0.

ENGLAND		Runs	Mins	Balls	4s		Runs	Mins	Balls	4s
B.C. Broad	c Marsh b Waugh	116	308	263	12*	not out	15	91	69	1
C.W.J. Athey	b Sleep	55	139	100	5	c Dyer b Hughes	12	26	20	2
*M.W. Gatting	c Waugh b Sleep	100	180	141	15	b Matthews	0	2	1	0
A.J. Lamb	c Matthews b Hughes	14	70	47	3	not out	9	59	48	1
D.I.Gower	lbw b Reid	38	61	41	5					
J.E. Emburey	c Dyer b Reid	49	161	118	6					
J.J. Whitaker	c Matthews b Reid	11	51	34	1					
†C.J. Richards	c Jones b Sleep	29	88	84	3					
P.A.J. DeFreitas	not out	4	53	84	—					
P.H. Edmonds	c Border b Sleep	13	26	28	1					
G.R. Dilley	b Reid	0	7	6	—					
Extras	(b4, lb14, w4, nb4)	26				(b2, lb1)	3			
		455				(2 wkts)	39			

*Plus 1 six

Fall: 112, 273, 283, 341, 361, 422, 439, 454, 455
21, 22.
Bowling: Hughes 30-8-82-1, Reid 28.4-8-64-4, Sleep 47-14-132-4, Matthews 23-1-102-0, Border 1-0-1-0, Waugh 19-4-56-1.

Hughes 7-2-16-1, Waugh 3-1-10-0, Matthews 8-4-10-1, Sleep 5-5-0-0.

Toss won by Australia
Man of the Match: A.R. Border

Test debuts: G.C. Dyer (Aus), J.J. Whitaker (Eng).
Umpires: A.R. Crafter & S.G. Randell

MATCH DRAWN

The Ashes are ours!

Wednesday 17 December

Poor Bruce French. He's having a rough time of it, something he doesn't deserve. He has swallowed his disappointment at losing his Test place, bounced back well and worked hard at his batting, ready to be able to play a full part for England if he should have a chance again on the tour. I've been impressed by his enthusiasm.

Yesterday, however, he reported pains in his chest and phoned Laurie this morning to say that they were worse. He was concerned enough for Peter Lush and Laurie to rush him to hospital before our early departure for Tasmania, largely to reassure Bruce that there was nothing seriously wrong. Laurie could not find anything muscular, and the doctors found no sign of infection because Bruce lacked a temperature and the usual signs that accompany a virus. The cause of the pain remained a mystery but the doctors were able to tell Bruce after a cardiograph check that there was nothing wrong with his heart. Bruce had been concerned on that score. He was certainly not well on our flight to Hobart, not helped by another rough landing which I gather is quite normal at this time of the year. Although he refused to rule himself out of tomorrow's four-day match against Tasmania, he looked a doubtful starter, which was a great pity. This game would be his last chance of first-class cricket on this tour with only the two Test matches and the two series of one-day internationals to come. The mood of the rest of the party was not helped by the pouring rain. This hasn't been the greatest start to an Australian summer. I can't remember a tour when the team have done so little sunbathing.

Thursday 18 December

Yesterday's heavy rain washed out the chance of play today, some of the water having got under the covering, soaking the wicket. In all honesty, I can't say that I am sorry. The rest of the boys feel the same way.

All are very tired and I put that down to having to play five days straight off in the Adelaide Test match. It is too much and I'm totally against the absence of a rest day after the third day. The Australians would like to play all their Test matches at home without a break because it serves television better, but the Test and County Cricket Board have insisted on a break wherever possible. The Australian players agree with us.

Not having had a break makes it very difficult for a captain, too, in trying to win Test matches on good pitches in the time-honoured way. That is by batting first, scoring a handsome total and then trying to force the opposition to follow on just as we did in the first Test in Brisbane.

Building a 550-plus total takes the best part of the first two days of the match. That leaves the third day to get among the opposition – either bowling them out before the close, or reducing them to such a state that there is the chance of enforcing the follow-on on the fourth morning. Either way the follow-on contains the risk of being in the field for the best part of three days and the players need that break after the third-day's play to recover.

In Brisbane I had no hesitation in asking the Australians to bat again late on the third day because I knew the following day was a rest day when the fast bowlers could put their feet up. I would have enforced the follow-on in Perth in the Second Test if I had had the chance early on the fourth morning – again in the knowledge my bowlers had rested completely the previous day.

As it turned out in Adelaide, the non rest day favoured us with Australia batting first. If we had been bowled out in our first innings on the third day and finished 210 or more runs adrift Allan Border would have been very tired, which would have given us the chance to build a large second-innings total with the pitch so good.

I can see why it is better for television to have Test matches played over five days straight. I can see that the financial gains to cricket may be greater with that system. But the feelings and the views of the players must also be taken into consideration. Make too many demands on them and the goods in the shop window become soiled. No, all Test matches should have a rest day.

Friday 19 December

We were all hoping that the rain and wash-out might have given Bruce French time to recover play against Tasmania today. Instead he was forced to go back into hospital yesterday to have further checks as the pain in his chest is still not easing. It would probably have done him more harm than good to have played anyway with the cruel wind blowing over the ground which is built halfway up an exposed hillside overlooking Hobart.

The wicket was still wet in places, and I had no hesitation in putting Tasmania in when I called correctly after David Boon had tossed. It was a vital toss to win in the conditions and by lunch Tasmania had been reduced to 36 for seven with Kent's swing bowler Richard Ellison – out here for the winter, doing his best to repair the damage with a stubbornn innings. Boon himself had dropped down the order in a bid to find his true touch away from the new ball but it did not make any difference. Everybody struggled against the bowling of DeFreitas, Foster and Small, the latter showing tremendous control into a strong wind with his two wickets costing eight runs coming from 14 overs. Daffy and Fozzy snapped four each as Tasmania were shot out for 79.

It was a good day too for Wilf Slack – known to all of us now as 'Bishop Tutu' – who had scored a half century by the close in putting us well ahead. It was certainly his best innings of the tour and it was nice to see the smile back on his face on the coach journey back to our hotel this evening.

Saturday 20 December

The disappointment today was in Wilf not being able to go on and complete his century, being 11 runs short he was finally out. We still finished the day well in command, however, ready to chalk up another victory against a state side.

The most remarkable innings of all came from John Emburey who scored all his 46 runs in boundaries with 10 fours and a six which left us wondering if that was some kind of a world record. The local statistician traced two occasions when batsmen had scored 42 all in boundaries but could not find anybody who had scored more. It helped us take 263-run first innings lead and by the evening we had taken three wickets before Tasmania had cut the deficit by 50 runs.

Sunday 21 December

We had the match all wrapped up soon after lunch, for a satisfying innings and 96 runs victory with me having my longest bowl of the tour taking three of the remaining wickets. I had not planned to use myself for any great length of time but the wind was so fierce blowing down the wicket, I thought it unfair to ask any of our front-line bowlers to bowl into it. It took a mighty effort to get up to the wicket and by the end of the spell my face was red and raw from the strength of the wind. There is talk in Tasmania of finding a more modern, up-to-date ground than this and if they do, I hope it is not so exposed.

It was very good to run into Richard Ellison again, a bowler I admire. He lost his form at home last summer when he switched his line from that required in the Caribbean to one more suitable for England. He now looks to be finding himself again. The Tasmanian officials and players spoke highly of his attitude and approach.

England XI v Tasmania
Played at Hobart, Dec 18, 19, 20, 21

Tasmania 79 and 167
England XI 342 for 9 dec (W.N. Slack 89)

England won by Innings and 96 runs.

We also bumped into Brian Davison, the former Leicestershire and Gloucestershire batsman who is now residing in Tasmania, and this evening he entertained many of the team to his house. My bowling stint had left me drained so I decided to spend a quiet evening dining in the revolving restaurant on the top of the Wrest Point Hotel. Quiet until the lads returned whereupon Peter Lush ousted the resident pianist in the piano bar and gave us his own version of 'Greensleeves'. I've heard better.

Monday 22 December

The big bonus from our stay in Hobart had been the rapid improvement in Ian Botham. Beefy's finances had improved as well from the casino in the hotel which is just off the lobby and packed every night. He had taken them for A$6,000 during his stay. I believe most of the team who had ventured into the casino had come out on top, although they made far more modest investments than Beefy who never does things by halves.

Whether his fortune on the tables had anything to do with the rapid improvement in his health, I don't know, but he had twice attended the nets in Hobart where he struck the ball without any apparent difficulty. Even better was the fact that he managed to bowl a few deliveries without feeling the rib injury, although they were very gentle efforts. It gave us hope that we might yet be able to play him in the Fourth Test in Melbourne, starting on Boxing Day, as an all-rounder.

At least it gave me the chance to include him in our side as we journeyed to Canberra for the one-day game against the Prime Minister's XI tomorrow – much to the delight of Prime Minister Bob Hawke who is a keen cricket fan. I told Ian he would have to bowl his ten overs and he agreed to give it a go.

This evening we spent a pleasant two hours with Bob Hawke on the lawns of the Prime Minister's Lodge, not far from the new Parliament building that is due to be completed in time for Australia's bicentenary in 1988. It was a relaxing time with Bob Hawke mixing freely with members of both sides, demonstrating his knowledge of the game.

I was very impressed, too, with 'Stork' Hendry who, at 91, is the oldest living Test cricketer, having played 11 times for Australia in the 1920s. He has a lively mind still and his conversation showed that he was well up with what was happening in cricket today.

Tuesday 23 December

The match itself proved an ideal run out for us, made all the better by our four-wicket victory against a strong Prime Minister's XI. We took the game seriously enough but the atmosphere was very relaxing in front of a largish crowd filling the pleasant tree-lined ground. I thoroughly enjoyed it.

The main benefit was being able to give Ian match practice, although he bowled his ten overs at a slow medium pace. He started off running in from only six paces and gradually moved out to eight or nine by the end when he found his rib was not hurting him. He even bent his back a couple of times to produce bouncers. It was a very critical time for us with Melbourne approaching.

Typically Ian made the first breakthrough when having South Australian Glen Bishop caught behind just after it had been announced that the tall, good-looking stroke-maker had been selected in Australia's 14-strong squad for the four-nation Perth Challenge one-day competition for the New Year. He and Mike Veletta, the Western Australian opener who had been on the Test tour of India, had given the Prime Minister's XI a good start in putting on 109 inside 23 overs, but we were able to peg them back after that. I was satisfied in limiting them to 240 for five off their 50

98

The England team with Australian Prime Minister, Bob Hawke

overs on a very good batting pitch. They did manage a late spurt when Allan Border arrived at the wicket and hit 41 but he paid for it. His cricketing gear had not arrived so he borrowed his pads and protective gear from David Gower but also used Ian Botham's heavyweight bat and confessed afterwards that his arms were exhausted carrying that solid chunk of timber around.

Apart from Allan Lamb failing to get going, I got everything I wanted out of our innings in knocking off our 241 victory target with 14 deliveries to spare – including getting Ian to the wicket. I had suggested that he should bat higher up the order than his normal number six position but Ian was happy to stay where he was. It took a little scheming to get him in long enough to play a decent innings, but David Gower gave me the opportunity with a delightful 68 which virtually assured we would make the runs in time. We had put on 50 together leaving victory some 60-odd runs away and giving me a chance to loft a few shots, offering a catch which brought Ian to the crease to provide the final decoration to the innings.

We could have wrapped it up with almost four overs to spare but for Ian's desire to fulfill a promise to Bob Hawke and hit a six. He wound himself up a couple of times against Border's gentle left-arm spin without being able to make the proper contact and was caught just inside the boundary next over when we needed only two more runs. He told me afterwards that he felt no reaction from his rib injury. There had been one twinge early on in his ten overs but nothing more and he declared himself fit to bat and bowl in the Melbourne Test, although I was a little concerned when he reported he would not be able to bowl more than 70 per cent of his normal pace. Micky and I decided to sleep on it before committing the England team.

There was no doubt that Ian was fit to play as a batsman, a fact that lifted the team on our return to Melbourne that evening where we started to think about Christmas for the first time. I, for one, had put the festive season out of my mind. It was occupied by the cricket, that had been pretty easy to do. Now the cricket was over for 48 hours, and it is not a pleasant time when separated from the family by 12,000 miles. I know it is worse for the families at home because there is no escaping the Christmas atmosphere for them. Out here it doesn't feel like Christmas despite the decorations in the streets and the number of Santa Clauses around. They appear out of place in the sunshine.

England XI v Prime Minister's XI
Played at Canberra, Dec 23

Prime Minister's XI 240 for 5 (50 overs) (M.R.J. Valetta 75)
England XI 241 for 6 (47.4 overs) (D.I. Gower 68)

England XI won by 6 wickets.

Wednesday 24 December

There was still a serious net session to go through this morning before we could fully concentrate on the Christmas activities planned, making last-minute purchases to complete our fancy-dress costumes for the Christmas lunch.

Ian was full of life at the nets, reporting no reaction to his match yesterday. After chatting to him we decided this evening to take the chance and include him in the side instead of James Whittaker.

We spent a considerable amount of time looking at the wicket this morning and were pleased to see it looked in better condition than the one we had experienced for the match against Victoria a few yards away. We thought it might help the pace bowlers on the first day and that encouraged us to take a more positive attitude. For some time I had been thinking of putting Australia in if I won the toss, convinced we had the bowlers to be able to bowl Australia out fairly cheaply – around the 250 mark – if there was some help in the pitch. To be on the safe side we also named Gladstone Small and Neil Foster in our squad when we announced it this evening.

The day was finished in Ian's room, a Christmas Eve party everybody attended. It was a good evening and there was no doubt the team was buzzing.

Thursday 25 December

This was undoubtedly the best Christmas Day I have spent with England overseas. I thought the one in India two years earlier would take some beating, but today was better.

Manager Peter Lush was partly responsible, in my opinion, in insisting we break with tradition and invite all the wives present to attend the team's Christmas Day lunch which had previously been a strictly male affair. It made the day as far as I was concerned, with the wives – now around ten in number – present as well as a few kids. It was more like Christmas at home and I enjoyed a spell feeding the latest addition to the Botham family, his 13-month-old daughter Rebecca.

The social committee under David Gower's guidance had worked wonders as

Relaxing with our families at Christmas

well in keeping the afternoon going and the fancy-dress costumes were the best I have seen, helped by the fact that we were in Melbourne where we could take advantage of some nearby fancy-dress shops. Daffy DeFraitas scooped the award coming as Diana Ross complete with slinky red dress that left little to the imagination! He had spent some days wondering whether he should shave off his moustache but decided the price was too high to pay, even in his attempt to be a Diana Ross look-alike.

For the fancy dress each player is issued with an initial and has to find an approporiate outfit. I was given 'm' and went as a musketeer, which I hoped the Australian spinners found suitable!

The morning started with the Press providing the team with a champagne party. It was a very pleasant affair, a time when any differences between us are forgotten, although those differences had grown far less in recent weeks. Christmas away from home is as painful for them as it is for us. Their party contained an entertaining 15-minute sketch which was played around a snoring figure in bed. My sleep-in was not going to be forgotten in a hurry.

Our own party followed, finishing around four which allowed time for a rest before a team meeting this evening where Micky and I both stressed the need for us to be positive in this match. Australia had to win the next Test, which meant that they had to take chances. We felt we could capitalise on any slip they may make and take the game ourselves to secure the series. Micky and I were confident they could be taken once they opened up. Being one down with two to go, they had to open up in this game.

The day ended with an appearance live into the Noel Edmonds Christmas Show, when many of us were linked with relatives in studios throughout England. I had a quick chat with my wife Elaine and my sons Andrew, four, and eight-month-old James. It was all too brief and we felt let down by the programme organisers who had promised our appearance would be in the first 15 minutes. Instead we were kept hanging around for an hour, some of the lads forced to stand throughout that period. It was a disappointing finish to what had been a most enjoyable day. It meant we all went to bed later than we wanted to with the heavy workload ahead.

Friday 26 December

An unbelievable day, simply unbelievable. The Fourth Test match, the series and the Ashes just handed to us if we can just keep our heads. A series of suicidal Australian batting strokes that were ridiculous against bowlers with the skill of Gladstone Small and Ian Botham, who took five wickets each, aided by some stunning catches by Jack Richards has got us to this position.

Australia were all out in two sessions for only 141 and by the close this evening we were handily placed only 46 runs behind with nine wickets left. I've had to pinch myself two or three times this evening to make sure I had not dreamt the whole thing. We now just have to guard against the danger of thinking the match is already won. It is essential we remain sharp. It is too big an opportunity to blow by complacency.

We had some long and hard thinking to do before the match, starting with finding a new-ball replacement for Graham Dilley. He shocked us this morning by saying he did not think he could get through five days on his dodgy right knee. It had swollen up again during the one-day game in Canberra with an excess of fluid, just as it had been doing after the two previous Test matches.

I had expected him to be fit and it was quite a surprise when he tried it out at the ground and then said it might not stand up to two days in the field. With Ian not 100 per cent fit, we could not take any chances.

That presented us with an extra headache. I had asked several of the senior players to have a look at the pitch with me and had made up my mind to bowl first if I was fortunate enough to win the toss. This wasn't a defensive move to keep our batsmen away from their bowlers on the first day; I had no worries about our batsmen being able to cope after making over 450 runs each time in our first innings in the three previous attempts. I felt it was the best way of bowling them out cheaply.

The first question the selectors had to decide was whether, in the absence of Dilley and the doubt about Ian, we should play the extra seam bowler and leave out a spinner. I was reluctant to lose either John or Phil and the others agreed we should stick to the balance we had used in the first two Test matches.

The next poser was in choosing between Gladstone Small and Neil Foster, who had both been taking wickets regularly against the state sides in between the Test matches. They were one and two in the Australian averages, Fozzy being slightly the more expensive but there was very little in it. In the end we opted for Gladstone on two grounds. He was the bowler who had made way for Phil DeFreitas' promotion at the start of the series and we felt that he could bowl tighter for longer periods than Fozzy. Fozzy was terribly disappointed, feeling that his batting might have opened up a place for him, but Gladstone was to prove us right in the end. Our decision was helped by an extraordinary one by the Australian selectors who sent Allan Border into the match with only four front-line batsmen, dropping Greg Ritchie. That decision convinced me we should bowl first if I won the toss. Fortunately I called correctly.

For the first hour there was little hint of the drama to come although David Boon had gone by then, his bat drawn to a fine delivery from Gladstone that moved away, offering Ian a regulation second-slip catch when the total was on 16. Gladstone was not as accurate as he might have been in his opening spell, more nervous of playing in front of a near 60,000 crowd than anything else. Daffy beat the bat without any luck but our initial new-ball thrust brought only one wicket.

I decided on a double change bringing John Emburey and Ian Botham into the attack at the same time. Immediately the match started going our way with Ian taking the wicket of Geoff Marsh with his fifth ball. It is incredible how he does it.

Daffy DeFreitas appeals for the wicket of Dean Jones

On the surface it appears a complete fluke yet it happens so regularly there is more to it than that. I am just grateful.

Twice in his first four deliveries Ian had dropped short, bowling very temptingly at his reduced pace. Each time Marsh had let the ball go but had practised the pull shot afterwards. I think he made up his mind that the next time Ian dropped one short he was going to have a go come what may. The next time was Ian's fifth ball. Only it was a little faster and a little wider of the off stump. Almost ideal for Marsh to square cut as he plays that stroke so well. He tried to pull it instead, got a top edge and Jack Richards held the catch above his head, clawing it down after a leap like a goalkeeper pulling the ball down from under the crossbar.

It was a wonderful effort and the next offering by the same combination was even better, coming as it did five minutes before lunch and seeing the back of Border. It was another shortish delivery Border shaped to cut but it moved into him off the wicket. The ball finished too close to Border for the shot he had in mind and he edged it for Jack to take a stunning catch diving to his left – his wrong side – in front of John Emburey at first slip.

Australia were 80 for three and lunch, for them, could not have been very appetising. I had the three wickets I wanted from the morning session, the one of Border being a bonus because their innings these days hinges around him. His dismissal simply knocked all heart out of them. The next seven wickets all went down between lunch and tea with the trio of Botham, Small and Richards seemingly taking on Australia all by themselves.

Gladstone was superb in his third spell, picking up four of the wickets. His line was immaculate on or just outside off stump and swinging the ball away from the right handers. He beat every batsman who faced him. Ian was pure Botham, teasing the batsmen into errors in picking up another three wickets. He varied his approach at the crease, disguised his pace – and risked his long hops.

Before he had finished there was one other remarkable catch by Jack Richards when Craig McDermott got a top edge with an attempted hook. It went a long way up and Jack sped off in pursuit immediately. So did Chris Broad from mid wicket and Gladstone from long leg. For a moment I thought there was going to be a nasty collision, leaving me three short for the rest of the game, but Chris and Gladstone appreciated Jack's positive, determined approach and backed off leaving the wicket-keeper to complete a diving catch at the end of a 25-yard long sprint.

Jack finished with five catches in an innings of an Ashes match to equal the haul achieved by Jim Parks on the 1965–66 tour and Bob Taylor in 1978–79. I was pleased for him because his promotion to Test status had not been received wholeheartedly by the media, who had largely sympathised with Bruce French. Even before his three remarkable catches he had caught the eye with two fine-leg side stops saving four runs each time. Most spectators favoured his sprint and catch off McDermott as the best, but we all thought the dive to hold Border's edge inches from the ground was superior. That was the one Jack was pleased with from the technical viewpoint.

Gladstone Small, whose 5 for 48 in the first innings won him the
Man of the Match award

My own bowling was limited to one over

Gladstone had finished with five wickets in an innings for the first time in his Test career. Ian Botham had done it for a remarkable 27th time to equal the Test record of Richard Hadlee. It was heady stuff but we had to make it pay.

Australia's previous lowest score at Melbourne had been 138 in the Centenary Test nine years earlier and they had hit back that day to bowl England out for 92. We had to make sure it did not happen this time and we were left with two hours to negotiate on the first day. I was worried because the pitch still offered sideways movement. I need not have concerned myself with Chris Broad and Bill Athey around.

They put on 58 before they were separated, Bill rather unfortunate to be given out leg before against a delivery we all thought pitched outside leg stump from left-arm seamer Bruce Reid. I joined Chris determined there would not be another breakthrough over the final 25 minutes and we finished on 95 for one. It could hardly have gone better.

Saturday 27 December

My jubilant mood of the previous evening was replaced with one of disappointment and frustration tonight at the end of the second day. We had been bowled out for 349 to give us a 208-run first-innings lead, but I couldn't help feeling we had left the door open for Australia to sneak in the back way and find a way out of the mess they were in after day one.

Our batting, in the main, was a big let-down after I had told the team that I was looking for us to be occupying the crease still at the end of the third day. There was a lack of discipline about it, a lack of commonsense which could still prove costly.

There were the exceptions. Another century by Chris – making three in successive Tests, joining a short list of English batsmen who have achieved that feat in an Ashes series. Jack Hobbs did it twice in 1911–12 and 1924–25 and Wally Hammond did it in 1928–29. Chris put the Broad name alongside those two cricketing giants. We were also saved by the tail wagging splendidly through John Emburey, Phil Edmonds and Gladstone Small making 62 between them at a time when Australia – having their best day in the field in the series – must have thought they had kept our first innings lead down to around the 150 mark.

Fortunately we got through the morning session without too much trouble. Starting the day trailing by 46 runs, we couldn't afford to lose early wickets and Chris and I managed to keep Australia out for the first two hours, reaching lunch at 163 for one, by which time we were in the lead by 22 runs. It had been hard going. Reid was again the pick of the Australian bowlers although Merv Hughes, in front of his own crowd and getting roars of encouragement whenever he ran in, bowled a great number of very useful deliveries.

I have to plead guilty to playing the first of the undisciplined strokes against the first ball I received after lunch. Reid dropped it short, I hooked it round off the middle of the bat but the contact was not firm enough to take it over the head of Merv Hughes who took a good catch at long leg. I cursed myself. I should have got the feel of the pitch again before striking out and I knew it was a bad example to set as I made the long walk back.

By tea we had lost another two wickets and were being rocked back a little as Australia's ground fielding improved too. Allan Lamb looked far from secure when he took over my place but he battled it through, seeing Chris depart when caught behind after his 328-minute stay for his 112. What a great selection the left-handed opener has proved to be.

Allan also saw David Gower depart after a disappointing innings, playing too loosely on a pitch offering the bowlers some help. He had been lucky to escape once in the over from leg spinner Peter Sleep when he made another attempt to hit him over the top and was caught at long-off.

It became worse after tea. Just when he looked to have found his touch Allan Lamb was caught behind and Ian Botham went the same way. When Jack Richards and Daffy DeFreitas fell, we were only 148 runs ahead. Fortunately the last three saw to it that the early work was not wasted. John Emburey and Phil

Edmonds added 30 for the last wicket before John drove a return catch to McDermott. Then Gladstone and Phil added another 30 for the last wicket – valuable runs. Gladstone really enjoys his batting. One off drive to the boundary was as good as anything anyone else produced all day. He followed that with a remarkable stroke when he started to give McDermott the charge, realised the ball was too far pitched up yet still managed to step back and cut it square with his bat only six inches off the ground.

The final ball of the day ended our innings. It was better than it might have been. Far worse than it should have been if only we had batted sensibly. I can't confess to being too happy at this moment. Our rash batting in Adelaide had let Australia back in with a chance and I feel now we have thrown away another opportunity of killing the Australian challenge stone dead.

Sunday 28 December

I don't think there will ever be another day in my cricketing life to match today. Certainly it has been the greatest moment since I won my first cap for England. The Ashes retained, Australia crushed inside three days, Elton John leading the champagne throwing in the dressing room. I can't imagine why I was so worried only 24 hours ago.

At the start this morning I could see no reason why the Australians should not have scored around 350 or so and been in a position to put us under a little pressure, especially if they managed one or two lucky breaks. By half an hour after tea it was all over. Australia all out for 194. England winners by an innings and 14 runs. The main reason for travelling 12,000 miles from England had been achieved. I was overjoyed. And so must have been every Pom in Australia this evening.

We were indebted to Australia's help. Before the match started Allan Border was quoted in every Australian newspaper as saying he wanted his batsmen to have a go and he would sooner go down fighting than lose all hope of regaining the Ashes by drawing the Test. During the first innings the Aussie batsmen appeared to take him too literally by the way they got out to a series of rash attacking strokes. I thought they would have realised their errors by the second innings, playing with more sense and appreciating they still had a chance. But it made little difference.

In only the fifth over Boon was edging Gladstone Small again to give me a catch at first slip. From that moment onwards it was just a question of chipping away, with the spinners taking over control this time on a pitch offering them some turn. They simply strangled the Australian batsmen into submission by their control so that the batsmen were never sure how to combat them.

If there was a moment that actually turned the match on the third day, it came when Gladstone was bowling to Border who stepped back and cut fiercely. It looked a four all the way until John Emburey took off to his right at third slip,

Chris Broad acknowledges applause after his third successive Test century

clutched it in his right hand and then closed his left one over it to make sure the ball did not pop out when he hit the ground. It was a superb piece of athleticism for such a big man.

Border and Geoff Marsh had put on 65 in 85 minutes following the fall of Dean Jones who had given me my second slip catch off the bowling of Daffy. They were looking dangerous, the two batsmen in the Australian side with the composure

Allan Border goes down fighting

and confidence to battle it through. With Border's departure I knew we had one end open as a result of their selectors giving their captain only four specialist batsmen.

The last main obstacle was removed when Marsh ran himself out, still clearly unsettled by an incident two balls earlier batting against John Emburey. He had thrust his left pad forward but not forward enough to counter the bounce as the ball rolled up his pad and on to his gloves to give Bill Athey an easy catch at short leg. We felt certain he had touched it but umpire Dick French turned down our appeals, while Marsh stayed there looking very embarassed. He apologised later saying that he knew he should have walked, but when French made no move to give him out, he stayed because of Australia's desperate position. It obviously unsettled him for Geoff is a very decent and straightforward character. Two balls later he drove the ball to Phil Edmonds at extra cover and set off for a run which was never on. By the time his partner Steve Waugh realised the danger Phil had the ball in his hand and his perfect return to Jack Richards gave Marsh no opportunity of reaching his ground.

England appeal in vain for the wicket of Geoff Marsh

John Emburey congratulates me . . .

and champagne flows in the dressing room

That was virtually curtains for the Aussies with the fielders now giving the bowlers immaculate support. Another smart piece of work between David Gower and Phil resulted in Peter Sleep being run out and the rest caved in with the last seven wickets going down for the addition of 41 runs, the last five falling for 25 runs in 10.4 overs after tea. The Ashes had been regained.

I missed the initial celebrations in the dressing room because of the immediate post-match television interviews. I felt for Allan Border then and couldn't help putting a consoling arm around his shoulder as we walked away together. He had tried really hard personally and I knew how he must have been feeling after my own experiences against India and New Zealand.

By the time I returned to the dressing room the celebration party was in full flow led by Elton who had been at the match every day. Waving a large Union Jack, he sprayed me with champagne until I was saturated. There was more champagne being sprayed than drunk but nobody cared. Alan Smith, the new Test and County Cricket Board chief executive had called in at Melbourne to watch the match and Doug Insole, chairman of the Overseas Tours Committee arrived in time to catch the last day. Nobody appeared more delighted than Phil Edmonds and Gladstone Small. I don't think I can ever remember Phil joining in so wholeheartedly, while the smile on Gladstone's face stretched from ear to ear. He had rightly been named 'Man of the Match' for his five wickets in his first innings,

A constant supporter on the tour, Elton John joins in the after-match celebrations

his score of 21 not out and the vital breakthrough with Border's wicket in the second.

It was some time before we cleared the England dressing room but that did not put a stop to the celebrations. Ian threw a victory party in his hotel room along with Elton John acting as disc jockey on the tape deck. Every member of the side was there which was good to see.

Ian has been superb throughout this tour, enjoying the success and working hard in so many ways, especially sharing his cricketing knowledge. His enthusiasm has been tremendous. We have had our differences in the past but I can't fault him this time and I also like to think the tour has been very good for him. What a night! What a day! Victory over Australia inside three days, the first time they have lost an Ashes game in Australia inside three days since 1901–02. Remarkable!

FOURTH TEST MATCH

Melbourne Cricket Ground, December 26, 27, 28

AUSTRALIA		Runs	Mins	Balls	4s		Runs	Mins	Balls	4s
G.R. Marsh	c Richards b Botham	17	69	46	2	(2) run out (Edmonds/ Richards)	60	213	141	6
D.C. Boon	c Botham b Small	7	20	11	1	(1) c Gatting b Small	8	21	21	—
D.M. Jones	c Gower b Small	59	153	136	6	c Gatting b DeFreitas	21	43	33	3
*A.R.Border	c Richards b Botham	15	42	26	2	c Emburey b Small	34	85	82	4
S.R. Waugh	c Botham b Small	10	44	30	—	b Edmonds	49	114	103	3
G.R.J. Matthews	c Botham b Small	14	75	50	1	b Emburey	0	7	7	—
P.R. Sleep	c Richards b Small	0	11	8	—	run out (Gower/Edmonds)	6	25	25	1
†T.J. Zoehrer	b Botham	5	13	7	1	c Athey b Edmonds	1	7	8	—
†C.J. McDermott	c Richards b Botham	0	6	4	—	b Emburey	1	16	14	—
M.G. Hughes	c Richards b Botham	2	14	15	—	c Small b Edmonds	8	10	8	2
B.A. Reid	not out	2	5	3	—	not out	0	4	4	—
Extras	(b1, lb1, w1, nb7)	10				(lb3, w1, nb2)	6			
		141					194			

Fall: 16, 44, 80, 108, 118, 118, 129, 133, 137, 141.

13, 48, 113, 153, 153, 175, 180, 185, 189, 194.

Bowling: Small 22.4-7-48-5, DeFreitas 11-1-30-0, Emburey 4-0-16-0, Botham 16-4-41-5, Gatting 1-0-4-0.

DeFreitas 12-1-44-1, Small 15-3-40-2, Botham 7-1-19-0, Edmonds 19.4-5-45-3, Emburey 20-5-43-2.

ENGLAND		Runs	Mins	Balls	4s
B.C. Broad	c Zoehrer b Hughes	112	328	255	9
C.W.J. Athey	lbw b Reid	21	74	57	1
*M.W. Gatting	c Hughes b Reid	40	171	118	2
A.J. Lamb	c Zoehrer b Reid	43	140	92	5
D.I.Gower	c Matthews b Sleep	7	21	17	1
I.T. Botham	c Zoehrer b McDermott	29	65	54	4
†C.J. Richards	c Marsh b Reid	3	32	14	—
P.A.J. DeFreitas	c Matthews b McDermott	7	20	14	—
J.E. Emburey	c&b McDermott	22	40	30	2
P.H. Edmonds	lbw b McDermott	19	66	49	1
G.C. Small	not out	21	41	36	2
Extras	(b6, lb7, w1, nb11)	25			
		349			

Fall: 58, 163, 198, 219, 251, 273, 277, 289, 319, 349.
Bowling: McDermott 26.5-4-83-4, Hughes 30-3-94-1, Reid 28-5-78-4, Waugh 8-4-16-0, Sleep 28-4-65-1.

Toss won by England
Man of the Match: G.C. Small

Umpires: A.R. Crafter & R.A. French

ENGLAND WON BY AN INNINGS AND 14 RUNS

Monday 29 December

Although everybody else had the day off today to recover from the celebrations I found myself under pressure to enlarge upon a remark I made at the post-match press conference when I said that there had been much of the England captaincy I had not enjoyed. The fact that I was being called upon to explain that remark was part of the reason.

There was no problem over the cricketing side of it, although I have had moments of near despair. That happens with Middlesex, too.

Moments like yesterday make up for the nights of gloom. No, the part of captaincy I don't find easy are the times when I can't be myself. I've found myself almost forced to carve out a new identity, having to be careful about every word I utter and not being able to relax and enjoy the free time with the other players as I would like because I was on call.

I'm young enough at the age of 29 to be doing the job for some years yet, as long as I can retain my batting form and England are successful. Yet I have my doubts whether I could get into a frame of mind to view the captaincy as a lengthy role – even after last night. The job as a whole is much more demanding than I ever thought it would be. And that is with having Peter Lush and Micky Stewart sharing more of the captaincy load than many other England captains have enjoyed. Or even permitted, in some cases.

Perth Challenge champions

Tuesday 30 December

I went book-hunting with a purpose this morning to buy a copy of *Winning Ways* by Dr Rudi Webster, the former Scotland, Warwickshire and Otago fast-medium bowler. That may sound a little strange considering we had just regained the Ashes but I wanted to refresh my memory.

I had read it before and found it very enlightening. There were a couple of chapters I thought I should read again before we tackled the four-nation Perth Challenge one-day competition being held to celebrate the start of America's Cup Year. Sadly the British entry *White Crusader* had already been eliminated after a very brave attempt to make the last four in the Challengers' series of races off Fremantle.

They had gone, but the West Indies and Pakistan had flown in to join Australia and us in the Perth competition. Each side was to play the others once with two points for a win, the top two in the final league placings going into the final. Pakistan were staying just for the ten days of the competition, the West Indies staying on for the triangular World Series one-day competition starting immediately after the final Test.

I wanted to read Rudi's book to make sure I got my thinking right for the Perth competition, particularly coming up against the West Indies who had given us such a torrid time in the Caribbean only eight or nine months earlier. I wanted the whole team to approach the game with a confidence built on winning the Ashes instead of thinking we were automatically booked for second place just because the West Indies had generally beaten us over the short course.

The way everything was coming together for us with every player improving as the tour progressed, I felt we might be able to pull off a victory. Certainly Micky Stewart was working hard on the rest of the team, preparing them mentally. We were given further encouragement about 15 minutes before we touched down at Perth on our evening flight from Melbourne when the pilot of our jet announced that Pakistan had beaten the West Indies by 34 runs in the opening round.

That caused quite a stir. Some two hours earlier, soon after take-off from Melbourne, the pilot had announced that Pakistan had been limited to 199 for eight off their 50 overs and we all assumed the West Indies would match that total quite comfortably. Instead they panicked, we were to discover later, following a horrible run-out mix-up between Viv Richards and Richie Richardson which cost them the wicket of the latter and they were bowled out for only 165 in 46.2 overs. It was a great win for Imran Khan's side, although they were helped by West Indies being without both Malcolm Marshall and Joel Garner who had sustained slight injuries.

Apart from proving that the West Indies could be beaten I tried to work out whether it was a good thing or not as far as we were concerned. We were next on the West Indies' schedule in four days' time and they would obviously be thirsting to restore their pride. Before then, however, we had to take care of our first opponents, Australia, on New Year's Day.

Wednesday 31 December

Our first task was to trim our 16-strong party by two to meet the requirements of the competition. Obviously only one wicket-keeper was going to be included – who had to be Jack Richards. We needed every bowler available in case of injury and we wanted James Whitaker because he could cover for any position in the top order. It meant, unfortunately, leaving out Bruce French and Wilf Slack. It hasn't been much of a tour for either of them as far as the cricket is concerned and I sympathise with them.

Australia had also named their squad bringing in all-rounders Simon O'Donnell and Ken Macleay as well as Victorian fast bowler Simon Davis who has a reputation for being one of the tightest new ball bowlers in one-day cricket in the country. The surprise, as far as we were concerned, was the axing of Greg Ritchie in favour of Glen Bishop largely on the grounds, I understand, that Ritchie was a little slow over the outfield for one-day cricket. Their one other change was bringing in New South Wales left arm bowler Mike Whitney for Merv Hughes, a move many in our side thought they might have made for the Melbourne Test.

We also had a problem to consider. More than half our squad had never sampled cricket under floodlights and Micky arranged a special 'sighting' session this evening after our nets. Playing when it is dark is no problem, especially with the white ball against the black sightscreens. It is the twilight period that causes difficulties.

As it happened we could not have a proper net session because the practice area wasn't really suitable, but we used the time waiting for the twilight zone well with a meeting where Micky and I stressed the competition could be won – the West Indies overcome – as long as we concentrated on the work we had been doing, bowled in the areas we wanted to bowl and had belief in our own ability rather than worrying about the opposition. Micky spoke very well and I could see some of the younger and newer players almost growing an inch as they grew in confidence during the talk.

With all that going on we had little time left to celebrate New Year's Eve although it wasn't a question of going to bed early with our match the next day not starting until 1.45 pm. Even so it was not until gone nine that I managed to get back into the hotel where I met an old footballing colleague from my days with Hendon Reserves waiting for me, Ray O'Callaghan. Ray has been in Australia for eight or

*The cricket ground at Perth under floodlight – a new experience
for over half our squad*

nine years and we saw the New Year in together – down in the disco area of our hotel along with members of the Pakistan, Australian and West Indies sides. It was quite a lively and enjoyable get-together.

Thursday 1 January

My main concern about our opening match against Australia was to try to keep the hold over Allan Border's side we had already established. I wanted to win the Perth competition because nothing breeds success better than success. But I also wanted to make sure there was no let up on the pressure on the Australians with the final Test at Sydney still to come.

After Melbourne Bobby Simpson, Australia's cricket manager, had said he thought the week in Perth was a good thing for his team because it would allow them a little breathing space, perhaps a chance to regain some lost confidence if they could win a couple of the matches. I was determined to keep them down. Fortunately the rest of the lads were of the same opinion judging by the way they performed today. Although the victory margin was 37 runs in the end, we actually beat Australia by a mile.

I was fortunate to win the toss which enabled us to bat in daylight. Chris and Bill did their stuff again with an opening partnership of 86 off the first 22 overs before being separated. Our control was emphasised by the Allan Lamb-Ian Botham partnership which realised 106 in only ten overs, Ian striking the ball with tremendous power.

119

Parachutists entertain the crowd during the lunch interval

I have seen Ian hit the ball farther than he did this afternoon, but I don't think I have ever seen him hit the ball more splendidly than one straight drive in an over against Simon Davis which cost 26 runs. He had driven the first two deliveries to the boundary causing Border to order his long off and long on so straight that they were hardly more than ten yards apart. Yet Ian connected so perfectly with the fourth ball of the over, neither fielder had chance to move before the ball bounced back off the boundary fence. The two sixes that followed were typical.

His performance made me happy after I had decided to change the batting order, dropping myself down. Ian is sometimes a little reluctant to move any higher than number six but I felt he must go to the wicket with at least ten overs remaining so that he had time to look at the bowling a little before starting his blasting operations. Allan Lamb also enjoyed the freedom of the one-day game. Some critics had suggested he might be left out after struggling a little in the Test series but you can't argue with his one-day average of 41 plus. There was never any danger of us leaving him out. The result was a total of 272 for six from the 50 overs.

We were always in control from that moment onwards, even though I made it a little tougher for us by dropping Dean Jones when he had made only 15. He went on to make 104, but he could not find a partner against our bowling and excellent fielding. That was the real key. Setting fields in one-day matches is always a worry but the bowlers made it simple for me by bowling exactly where I wanted them to.

England v Australia
Played at Perth, Jan 1

England 272 for 6 (49 overs) (B.C. Broad 76, I.T. Botham 68, A.J. Lamb 66)
Australia 235 (48.2 overs) (D.M. Jones 104)

England won by 37 runs.   Man of Match: I.T. Botham

Friday 2 January

The wicket we had used last night had been perfect for one-day cricket. It favoured the batsmen, the bounce was even but it also had pace to help the ball on to the bat. Australia made better use of it today when they batted first against Pakistan, Dean Jones scoring a second successive century in helping his side reach 273 for six. Incredibly, Australia lost to go out of the competition after just two days. Long after the close I was trying to work out why. They certainly looked drained of confidence and I find it hard to understand why their bowlers still bowl in the wrong place for one-day matches despite all the experience they have had: too often they are guilty of bowling the good length ball, which is often much easier to score off in limited-overs cricket than one short of a length or well pitched up. It seems they have not learned the lessons of the past.

Pakistan appeared to have no chance when they lost their first five wickets for

96 of which Qasim Omar contributed 67 runs with a flurry of boundaries. By then they had used up 21 overs. When Imran Khan fell nine overs later with the score on 129 the Australians must have thought it was all over, Pakistan then needing 145 off the last 20. They made it with one ball to spare thanks to a group of players who were strangers to me in all-rounder Manzoor Elahi, left-arm spinner Asif Mujtaba, wicket-keeper Salim Yousuf and, finally, their two left-arm fast bowlers Wasim Akram and Saleem Jaffer.

When there were only four overs left Australia still appeared favourites with Pakistan needing to score at 10 an over but Asif chipped the ball with some wristy strokes neatly into the open spaces between the fielders inside the circle and those protecting the boundary. I am not surprised that Allan Border couldn't trust himself to speak to the media afterwards. He must have felt really sick. Dean Jones couldn't have been feeling much happier scoring centuries on successive evenings and finishing on the losing side each time.

Saturday 3 January

What a day! We have beaten the West Indies for only the sixth time in 23 matches and secured a place in the Perth finals against Pakistan although there were still two qualifying matches left.

It really was a marvellous performance with the West Indies back at full strength, Malcolm Marshall and Joel Garner having recovered from their injuries. We also had the worst of the conditions too. The first three matches had been played on the same stretch of turf offering plenty of runs. Today they switched the match to the other side of the square where the pitch was still a little damp, offering too much bounce and movement to the faster bowlers – as if the West Indian attack needs any assistance. It wasn't a good one-day pitch.

To conquer the West Indies on that surface was really something in my book. We did it because our bowling and fielding was first class again. And because of the courage of Allan Lamb and Jack Richards who took control with the bat when we were deep in trouble. We found ourselves ten for two before the fourth over had finished, with Chris Broad having a rare failure and Bill Athey joining him in the dressing room – the two men who had been giving our innings such perfect starts. That soon became 35 for three when David Gower fell, 67 for four when Courtney Walsh found the outside of my bat and 96 for five in the 25th over – the halfway mark – when Ian Botham top edged a pull against off spinner Roger Harper and was caught at square leg.

I thought then we might struggle to make much more than 150 but Allan and Jack played magnificently in adding another 60 runs off the next 11 overs, taking advantage of Harper's ten-over spell. Even then it took a remarkable catch to separate them when Allan cut Marshall hard and high only for Harper to leap in the air, stick out his right hand and hold a ball which must have been eight foot above the ground at the time. It had looked a certain four.

Allan's 71 had taken 108 balls and Jack scored at an even faster rate in making his 50 off 62 balls before he was out when caught behind. We managed to use up all our overs, finishing on 228 for nine, a score I would have quite happily settled for at the start of the innings given the condition of the pitch. It gave us a good chance as long as our bowlers could bowl in the slot. They did just that superbly to get us home by 19 runs with 10 balls to spare.

It was still hard going although we started well by sending back Desmond Haynes, Gordon Greenidge and Richie Richardson with only 50 on the scoreboard in 14 overs. Then Viv Richards staged a recovery along with Gus Logie in a 53-run stand until he was caught on the boundary by Chris Broad sweeping at John Emburey, a good catch this one with the ball coming out of the setting sun. Jeff Dujon then took over and it looked to be going the way of the West Indies when they started their last ten overs needing 60 to win with six wickets left, Logie and Dujon growing in confidence. We needed a breakthrough desperately. Phil

Jack Richards airborne

Viv Richards feels the heat in Perth

Edmonds had taken some stick so I brought back Graham Dilley one over early and he wrapped the match up for us with a four for seven return in his next 22 deliveries. He was almost unplayable, bowling as well now as I have seen any England fast bowler perform in the ten years I have been associated with the team. There can't be many better in the world at the moment as a genuine fast bowler with the ability to swing the ball either way. He bowled Dujon who was making room to cut, had Logie caught behind driving against his away swinger, brought one back to scatter Malcolm Marshall's stumps and then saw Michael Holding caught at long on desperately throwing the bat. With John Emburey having Courtney Walsh leg before two overs later, it was all over.

It was a victory for positive thinking, Micky's coaxing and cajoling paying off. I admit we caught the West Indies when they were a little rusty having not played a match for three weeks or so since finishing their tour of Pakistan. It showed a little with Marshall bowling three wides in his first over and Garner bowling five no-balls in all. Yet the West Indies have such talent it doesn't take them long to get into form and they had played one match against Pakistan. We had a drink or three this evening.

I celebrate a place in the Perth Challenge final after beating the West Indies

England v West Indies
Played at Perth, Jan 3

England 228 for 9 (50 overs) (A.J. Lamb 71, C.J. Richards 50,
J. Garner 5 for 47)
West Indies 209 (48.2 overs) (A.L. Logie 51)

England won by 19 runs.   Man of Match: G. Dilley

Sunday 4 January

With ourselves and Pakistan having beaten the West Indies and Australia it left those two countries fighting today to avoid finishing bottom of the four-team table. That role fell to Australia. They were outclassed by a West Indies side determined to stop the rot although they were without Malcolm Marshall again. Instead the Australians tasted Tony Gray's style, sharing the new ball with Joel Garner after the West Indies had 255 for eight based on a solid Gordon Greenidge century.

The Australian batsmen just didn't take to Gray, the lanky bowler Surrey signed in an emergency in 1985 when Sylvester Clarke suffered a back injury. Both his bounce and that obtained by Garner on the lively wicket upset the Australian batsmen – and the umpires. The Australian authorities are making a determined bid to cut out the amount of short pitched bowling in cricket in general and one-day internationals in particular. They have made the square-leg umpire responsible for signalling no-balls for any delivery that goes through above the shoulder height of a batsman standing normally at the crease. Both Garner and Gray offended – much to their annoyance although Allan Border complained afterwards that the umpires should have been even more strict. I thought the no-ball ruling was very sensible: I know the West Indies felt hard done by, but as it happened it was their batsmen who let them down rather than their bowlers. Certainly it made the cricket more attractive to watch – as well as play.

Australia just couldn't cope. They were all out for only 91 in 35.4 overs with Steve Waugh the only batsman to reach double figures, Gray claiming three for nine in 7.4 overs. The West Indies had got home by a comfortable 164 runs.

Far from the Perth Challenge competition proving a relief as Bobby Simpson had hoped, it had turned into a nightmare for the Australian side, putting even more pressure on them, although I didn't like the way the Australian fans booed their team. They didn't deserve that. Yet the way the Australians did fold so quickly made our victory the day before even more creditable.

Monday 5 January

This was not a very satisfactory day all round despite the fact that we overcame Pakistan in our final qualifying match which had been turned into a dress rehearsal for the actual final in two days' time.

We almost made a mess of matching Pakistan's 229 for five before getting in by three wickets with only two balls to spare. We were involved in one extraordinary scene when Pakistan batsman Rameez Raja was run out off a no-ball, saw Chris Broad denied yet another century by a debatable umpiring decision and produced our worst fielding display of the series for which I was partly responsible in failing to pick up two balls cleanly early in the afternoon.

The Rameez incident was curious; it was our turn to be booed this time although I thought it was unfair because we had done nothing wrong. It happened soon after we had split the Pakistan openers Shoaib Mohammad and Qasim Omar after they had put on 61 in 17 overs, Qasim being bowled cutting at Ian Botham. We had used the match to give Neil Foster a run in place of Graham Dilley who was being rested. Unfortunately Neil broke during his fourth over, straining his left knee, and I had to fill in as a bowler.

With Pakistan on 98 for one, we desperately needed a wicket to prevent them building a solid base for a slog and I thought I had got one when Rameez Raja tried to turn me on the leg side but dollied up a simple catch to Bill Athey stepping a few paces forward at mid-wicket. My jubililation was short lived as I heard umpire Tony Crafter's 'No-ball' shout and I stood at the end of my follow through, head bowed staring into space in my disappointment.

Rameez was just as disappointed and confused as I was. He obviously did not hear the no-ball shout and didn't spot Crafter's outstretched right arm either, following the flight of the ball into Bill Athey's hands as soon as he made contact. While I stood in the middle of the pitch with my head down, Rameez started to walk towards ther dressing room thinking he was out. Bill paused with the ball in his hands until Jack Richards shouted 'throw it' and then whipped off the bails. Rameez, suddenly aware that it had been a no-ball when Shoaib warned him, had turned to make his ground again but was out by almost half the length of the wicket. It was the shout from Jack that brought me back to reality just in time to see umpire Dick French at square leg give Rameez out.

I realised something strange had happened but it was not until the interval between the innings that I discovered Rameez should not have been given out under Law 38.2 which says a batsman can only be run out off a no-ball if he is attemping a run. Clearly Rameez had not been doing that. He had started to walk back as soon as he had seen the ball in Bill's hands and it was his ill fortune that the dressing room area happened to be behind the bowler's end. If it had been behind him he would have been perfectly safe because he would not have walked out of his crease.

It was a media inquiry that first alerted me to the fact that umpire French had made an error and I was also asked whether I had considered calling Rameez back. I had not because we had not done anything wrong and I was pleased at the end of the match when the Pakistan captain Imran Khan said there should be no blame attached to us in any way. The initial fault was Rameez not hearing the no-ball shout or spotting umpire Crafter's outstretched hand. The error was made by the umpires in not knowing the rules.

The one other problem we had with the Pakistan innings was controlling Javed Miandad who went on the attack to boost their scoring after Shoaib, the son of Hanif Mohammad, had taken 40 overs scoring his 66. It was too slow to give Pakistan the total they would have liked, especially as we were back playing on the good batting strip.

Javed Miandad in full flow

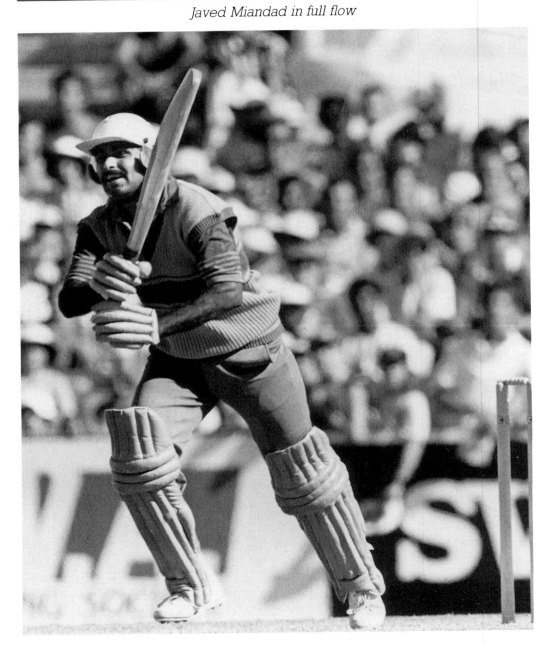

Once again our winning platform was set down by Chris and Bill in putting on 104 for the first wicket inside 27 overs. We just had to take it steady over the rest of the course. There was no need to take any risks. We did though, and almost paid the penalty. Perhaps we were not as switched on as we should have been, knowing that we were already in the final, although I had done my best to make sure the lads didn't adopt a 'never mind, we'll be all right on the day' approach.

It began to look a little dicey when we slipped to 199 for five in the 45th over with Imran bringing himself and Wasim Akram back into the attack. That was when I was run out, not taking enough care. An over later Jack Richards went the same way to leave us 204 for six with another 27 runs wanted with 27 balls left.

There should not have been any problem with Chris still at the wicket pacing his effort perfectly and I thought we would win it with at least one over to spare. Then came a tragic dismissal when Chris was on 96. He played a stroke against Imran, seemed nowhere near the ball as it went through around waist high but wicket-keeper Yousuf and Imran went up for a catch which was given.

Poor Chris was dumbfounded as he walked back to the dressing room without his job completed. It was one of the slowest returns I've seen, although he controlled his feelings well. That increased the pressure on us before Daffy DeFreitas and John Emburey calmly scored the winning runs. It gave us a psychological advantage for the final and it allowed us to look at their batsmen. In all a very worthwhile exercise.

England v Pakistan
Played at Perth, Jan 5

Pakistan 229 for 8 (50 overs) (Shoaib Mohammad 66, Javed Miandad 59)
England 232 for 7 (49.4 overs) (B.C. Broad 97)

England won by 3 wickets.   Man of Match: B.C. Broad

Qualifying Table:

	P	W	L	Pts
England	3	3	–	6
Pakistan	3	2	1	4
West Indies	3	1	2	2
Australia	3	–	3	—

Tuesday 6 January

The suspicion arose today that Australia's selectors had boobed badly in naming their 12 for the final Test in Sydney starting on Saturday. The make-up of the 12 suggested they might have picked the wrong man when they included 30-year-

129

old off spinner Peter Taylor from New South Wales, a player so unfamiliar to the Australian public, he soon became known as Peter Who? He was the main topic of conversation this evening when all four teams attended an official dinner. Nobody in our party had heard of him, which was not surprising considering he had not made his first-class début until 12 months ago and had played only four times for New South Wales in the Sheffield Shield competition, and just once this season, over this last weekend against Tasmania.

He had taken only one wicket in the rain-ruined game in Newcastle so there was nothing in that performance to make the selectors pick him. The suspicion that there had been an administrative error in naming the team was strengthened by the fact that vice captain and opening batsman David Boon had been dropped and there was no other recognised opener in the 12 although Mark Taylor, a burly left-handed New South Wales opener had been widely tipped. The suggestion was that somebody had got an initial wrong and P. Taylor named rather than M. Taylor. True or not, it caused some merriment at the reception.

There was also confusion in the Australian camp over the appointment of the vice captain. Dirk Wellham, the New South Wales right-hand batsman and captain, had been recalled to the Test 12. He is the most successful Sheffield Shield captain, having won the title for his state for the last two seasons and it was assumed he would be appointed Border's deputy in the absence of Boon. Instead, some 12 hours after the names of the 12 had been released, the Australian Cricket Board announced that Geoff Marsh was to take over, although he had no first-class leadership experience. Australian media men at the dinner told me Wellham had been vetoed by the board because of his strong connections with the launching of the rebel Australian side to South Africa two years ago. Whatever the truth, it showed that all was not quite as happy as it should be within the Australian camp and that could only be good for us.

Wednesday 7 January
Champions again, this time of the Perth Challenge. It is the first time, I was told afterwards, that England have won a one-day tournament with more than two countries involved. The thing that pleased me most about the five-wicket victory over Pakistan was our professional attitude.

We were determined. We applied ourselves to the task. Everybody knew what they had to do and did it perfectly. The result was another thoroughly splendid bowling performance backed up by first-class catching and ground fielding. Bill Athey, I thought, was brilliant. Only Javed Miandad managed to thwart us, for the second time, but his lone effort was never enough as we held him to 77 not out and Pakistan to 166 for nine.

We were in control from the moment that Graham Dilley bowled Shoaib with his fourth ball and then Bill set the standard for catching with a diving effort at mid-

Dilley bowls Shoaib Mohammad

wicket to hold Rameez Raja. This time there was no mistake. I thought David Gower's one-handed effort at extra cover to hold a Manzoor Elahi drive against Gladstone Small was one of the best. High in quality also was the one Jack Richards took off my bowling, standing up to take an edge when Imran Khan tried to cut. It was a good reaction catch. Come to think of it, my catch at first slip to claim the last wicket to fall, that of Wasim Akram was a pretty good one too. A diving catch to my left to scoop the ball only a few inches from the ground. I couldn't let Bill down!

There then were still 54 deliveries to go but so well did Javed farm the bowling that last man Salim Jaffer faced only five of them – including the last two of the innings. I wasn't particularly concerned because Javed was never able to break completely free as he can do.

The start of our reply was not without incident with poor Chris Broad the victim again. We had lost Bill Athey in Imran Khan's second over when he was caught behind. Then, in the next over from Wasim, wicket-keeper Yousuf went up for a leg-side catch against Chris who had started to play at a delivery that was going down but then checked his stroke. The ball actually changed direction when striking Chris just above his waist.

A happy moment for a captain: I show off the Perth Challenge trophy

Seeing Yousuf go up for the catch, Akram joined in while Chris stood absolutely astounded at the crease for a moment. Umpire Dick French made no move. Yousuf and Wasim looked deeply upset and Chris started to walk away towards square leg in disgust, taking five or six steps. That prompted another appeal from Wasim who thought Chris was starting to walk and umpire French took the same view – as he later confessed to me – and raised his finger. It was an unfortunate decision. French clearly did not know what had happened and was only guessing, which was wrong. If he was unsure he should have made only one decision – not out. Chris was obviously deeply upset but even he had to see the amusing side later when Dick French approached him and said 'If you're still talking to me, can I have your autograph?'

We didn't think it funny at the time when we were seven for two but David, Allan and myself took us within reach of Pakistan's total leaving Ian to finish the job with almost ten overs to spare.

I felt it was a good job thoroughly well done and there was a very satisfied air in the dressing room as we had yet more victory champagne, although none of us got as excited as we had done at Melbourne ten days earlier in winning the Ashes.

During the Perth Challenge everybody had contributed again. Allan Lamb returned to form, very keen to play even when he strained a thigh. He was not going to give in. David Gower found his touch after looking a little out of it during the previous fortnight. I managed to chip in with runs when it mattered and the bowlers all deserved medals for their control.

Phil DeFreitas was especially quick in the first meeting with Pakistan when I gave him the new ball in place of the rested Graham Dilley. I couldn't understand where he had got that extra zip from until Ian Botham told me that just as Phil was leaving the dressing room to go on the field he heard one of the Channel 9 television commentary team describe him as 'medium paced'. Phil apparently muttered all the way to the middle, 'I'll show them'. And he did. There was nothing medium about him that night. It was that type of spirit that had spread through the whole party.

England v Pakistan
Played at Perth, Jan 7

Pakistan 166 for 9 (50 overs) (Javed Miandad 77*)
England 167 for 5 (40.1 overs) (M.W. Gatting 49, A.J. Lamb 47)

England won by 5 wickets.   Man of Match: Javed Miandad

A classic finale

Thursday 8 January

Back across Australia from Perth to Sydney for the final Test match on Saturday. I must admit I am getting bored of flying and the worst section is still to come with the one-day international tournament to follow. I am not alone in feeling this way. The travelling is beginning to get everybody down as is living out of suitcases in the hotel life. At least on the four-hour flight I had time to reflect on and take stock of the Pakistan side. It will be tough in England during the summer; there are certainly no easy touches in Test cricket these days.

They may however be short of a spinner to support leg-break wizard Abdul Qadir who missed the Perth competition because of injury. There they turned to 20-year-old left-arm spinner Asif Mujtaba for the one-day internationals; we didn't really have much of a look at him as a bowler, although he appeared a useful batsman, as are most Pakistan and Indian players brought up on slow, bounceless tracks where the ball does not often deviate off the seam.

In terms of batting they will be a threat with the cavalier approach of Qasim Omar, the stroke play of Rameez Raja and the all-round ability of Javed Miandad, not to mention Imran Khan himself who will want to make an impression having announced his retirement from Test cricket at the end of this year.

The pace bowling will be quite testing, too. Imran is a particularly aggressive bowler, especially in English conditions, and I was quite impressed by left-arm fast bowler Wasim Akram in Perth. He is a little quicker than he appears and has the ability to bring the ball in against the right-handed batsman. They have another left-arm fast bowler in Saleem Jaffer, who is rather like Australia's Bruce Reid in that he tends to push the ball across the right-handed batsman. Only Jaffer is not so good. They will take some beating at home.

Friday 9 January

We had to take a rather painful decision this evening to leave Phil DeFreitas out of the side for tomorrow's match. Painful because Daffy did not deserve to be omitted, especially after the way he bowled in Perth. He perhaps hasn't taken the wickets he might have done in the last two or three Test matches but he has been unlucky and chipped in with vital wickets to help us achieve breakthroughs.

The problem was we had so many players in form at the same time. After the way he had bowled in the Melbourne Test, there was no way that Gladstone Small

134

would be left out and we had to find room again for Graham Dilley who had proved both his fitness and form during the Perth one-day competition.

With the Sydney wicket likely to take turn – Australia had won four of their last five Test matches played there through their New South Wales spinners Bob Holland, Greg Matthews and Murray Bennett – we obviously had to include our two. That meant no room for Daffy, but both Micky and I took extra care to explain to him that we were not dissatisfied in any way. He'll be playing in a lot of Test matches in the future.

We did not have time for our usual pre-Test dinner this evening because of a reception but no-one needed reminding this time what was required of them. There had been some suggestion that, with the Ashes won, we might not take this game quite so hard but I don't think there is any danger of that. Everybody seemed quite determined that we were going to come out of the series 3–0.

Saturday 10 January

Up until the last two matches in the Perth competition I had been perfectly content with the umpiring standard in the international matches. There had been a couple of leg before decisions that I thought we should have had particularly in the Perth Test, but we had also escaped a couple of times ourselves.

Tony Crafter and Steve Randell had particularly impressed us, both with the correctness of their decisions and the easy relationship they had with the players. They were friendly, approachable, easy to talk to on the field, standing up well to the strain of having their every decision replayed on the giant screens now dominating the grounds at Sydney, Melbourne and Perth.

They were having a tough season with the number of international games played in Australia in addition to officiating in the Sheffield Shield. Perhaps the pressure was getting to them, for more errors were starting to creep into their game. There was one decision today which stopped us dominating the opening day of the Test. I hope it doesn't prove crucial.

I was still reasonably content, with Australia finishing the day on 236 for seven after Allan Border had won the toss. We might easily have bowled Australia out for less than 200 if Dean Jones had been given out when he was on five. It irked us all to see him still there at the close propping up Australia with 119 against his name.

Graham Dilley had given us our customary early breakthrough when stand-in opener Greg Ritchie had proved as vulnerable as David Boon, falling leg before when the score was on eight. Australia had moved on to 27 with Jones struggling to assert himself when he attempted to glance Gladstone Small, the ball brushing the face of Jones' bat on its way through for Jack Richards to take a good diving catch to his left down the leg side. There was no doubt, as far as those of us in the close-catching position were concerned, that Jones had touched it. Gladstone was equally convinced but umpire Randell turned down our appeals just seconds before the big screen beyond the famous Hill area of the Sydney ground showed an action replay which confirmed our suspicions.

Umpire Randell, the youngest in Australia's Test history – he was only 28 when

Dean Jones goes on to 119 after a lucky escape

Jack Richards at full stretch

he first stood three years ago – is quite an outgoing character. I found myself walking off alongside him at the lunch break and I said to him jokingly 'Try and have some carrots for lunch, Steve.' Carrots were actually on our lunch menu and when we walked on to the field again for the afternoon Randell walked over to me with a half-bitten carrot wrapped up in a napkin!

The afternoon was the start of a great session for us inspired by some more excellent bowling from Gladstone. He had already claimed one wicket in his long opening spell when seeing Geoff Marsh edge a first-slip catch to me. Then he really turned it on after lunch, keeping the ball just outside the off stump to the right-handed batsmen and just moving it away, catching them in two minds whether to play at the delivery or leave it alone.

He had the chance to get at the new right-handers when Border turned Phil Edmonds to Ian Botham at backward short leg. That was the cue for Gladstone to dominate the others, held up only by Jones scoring his second successive century against us, following his 104 in the one-day game in Perth.

In 17 deliveries Gladstone had Dirk Wellham, Steve Waugh and Peter Sleep all caught behind for the cost of 16 runs. For good measure he added the wicket of Tim Zoehrer after tea. I really couldn't complain too bitterly despite the Jones decision, because after seeing the replay we looked distinctly fortunate to have removed Waugh. These things have a way of evening out in the end.

It's always a relief to see the back of Allan Border

Sunday 11 January

With new boy Peter Taylor partnering Jones and only Merv Hughes and Bruce Reid to come, I left the hotel this morning convinced we would have Australia all out for around the 250 mark again and would be well on our way towards a 500 total by the evening, ready to chase after another innings victory. Instead I came back deeply depressed with us on 132 for five, more than 200 runs behind.

I thought we had blown it on the most frustrating day of the series for us. Frustrating because Taylor defied us for 84 minutes on his Test début and then Hughes, whose batting is regarded as a bit of a joke even by Australians, stayed around for almost two hours helping Jones build his side's total to 343, Jones himself remaining unbeaten on 182. Neither of the tail-enders used their bats very often. It was more a question of sticking out their front leg, getting it as far down the wicket as possible and smothering the danger from John Emburey and Phil Edmonds, the pitch not fast enough to cause them any real problems. We also felt that Jones had another escape, looking plumb in front against Emburey when he had made 127 but McConnell found some fault in our appeal. Instead of us batting before lunch as I expected, we were kept hanging around until half an hour before tea, with disastrous consequences.

It is always a worry going in to bat after tail-enders have stayed around making it look easy. Spectators expect the same from genuine batsmen, without taking into account they are up against a new ball in the hands of fresh bowlers. By tea we had lost three for 17. Rather unluckily, I thought: Chris Broad and Bill Athey getting out not playing shots while I fell leg before although I was convinced the ball was missing leg stump.

Bill was unfortunate as he tried to leave alone a delivery from Hughes, the ball just brushing his glove to give a catch behind. Chris, so intent on getting a fourth century in successive Tests, offered no stroke to a good ball that pitched middle and held up enough to take off stump but for Chris' pad. Fortunately for us David was in wonderful form again, stroking the loose ball superbly, but we also lost Allan Lamb and Ian Botham before the close. Allan had helped pull us round and then became the first Test victim of Peter Taylor, who was fast becoming a nuisance to us. A new boy and off spinner to boot, was just too much for Ian to resist.

He was keen to dominate him from the start, to try to test Taylor's mental toughness, but then Both discovered that the hard way. He steered the first two balls he received from Taylor to the boundary. In the next over he clobbered him for a huge six over long on that threatened to come through our dressing room window. Another half a dozen deliveries and Ian was caught at short leg. Disappointing for everybody – except the Australian team.

My mood was lightened this evening by dinner with Elton John who really is a marvellous sports fan. He's been a great boost to us on this tour, attending every match he can, very seldom missing a ball. He has shared our great moments and cheered us up when things haven't gone as they should, he's a regular visitor to our dressing room and is also staying in the same hotel in Sydney. The Watford

*Peter Taylor on his Test debut at Sydney – 6 for 78 and the
Man of the Match award*

chairman, who is going on to watch the Australian Open Tennis Championships after the Test, is also a fair man. He is a frequent – and welcome – visitor to the Australian dressing room. It was a delightful evening.

Monday 12 January

I was able to relax again this evening at a barbecue with an old friend, Gavin Robertson, a player I used to coach during my grade cricket days with Balmain. The half lamb on the spit, beef and pork tasted much better thanks to John Emburey and Jack Richards who have put us back in the Test. They've done it as batsmen, and not their usual trade. David Gower, who had been 62 not out overnight, did not last long this morning much to Australia's relief. They thought he should have been out leg before in the last over yesterday. So did David when he watched the action replay on the screen. 'It must have been going under,' he told wicket-keeper Zoehrer, whose response was not so funny.

With only 142 on the board, leaving us 201 behind and six wickets down, I thought we would be fortunate to reach 200. Instead we managed to climb to within 68 runs of Australia's total and claim two wickets in the final session.

It was a courageous performance from John who hates losing as much as I do. He had made only seven when he made a sharp turn going for a second run and strained his groin. He said later it was a good job it was his second run and not Jack's otherwise he would have been even more upset. After one more delivery and running – or rather limping – a single, he waved for Bill Athey as a runner. Both he and Jack were fighting off the Australian spinners in the way the Australian tail-end kept us at bay, frustrating them by padding away anything pitched off the stumps with the left foot way down the wicket, safe in the knowledge that Australian umpires will not normally grant leg before decisions unless the feet are around the crease. Stretching such a long way forward was painful for John but he ignored it for three and a half hours before he was last out for 69, only six runs short of his Test best score.

Jack was with him for more than two hours in adding 71 for the seventh wicket and Gladstone put in another heroic performance with the bat in staying almost an hour while 51 runs were added for the ninth wicket. Both got out taking a swing against Peter Taylor, which gave the unknown Australian off spinner six for 78 on his Test début, a fine effort. He was a little fortunate; we gave him three or four wickets and he was able to bowl without being under pressure as a result of our poor start. I thought he bowled too many loose balls which escaped punishment because we were concentrating on defence.

Yet Taylor showed a great deal of potential and maturity. He also bowled a large number of good deliveries, kept his head and you can't do much better than finish with six wickets on your Test début. John Emburey was quite impressed with him, particularly the pace he bowled at to get the best out of a slow pitch. It did seem strange that he was 29 before New South Wales turned to him for the first time but spinners often mature later than fast bowlers. It takes time to learn the art properly and, at 30 now, he can still have a Test future.

The finish of our innings left Australia with just over two hours to start their second knock and we made the best use of it although Border looked in top form. He helped Australia into a 142 overall lead by the end of the day, after we had dismissed both Geoff Marsh and Greg Ritchie. With a little luck after tomorrow's rest day, we could be left with a 250 victory target and I fancy us getting there.

Tuesday 13 January
Our position allowed me to have a thoroughly enjoyable rest day which started with a game of golf with Richie Benaud.

The rest of the party were treated to a trip across Sydney by Bollinger, who were sponsoring a charity event, ending up with a game of beach cricket at Watson's Bay outside Peter Doyle's famous fish restaurant. I was able to finish golf in time to join in the beach cricket, although the sand was so crowded there was only a narrow avenue left in the end for the ball to be bowled amid the group of onlookers.

Inevitably the afternoon ended with people being tossed into the surf all in good fun. It was a relaxing day in preparation for the two hard days of cricket left. I was impressed by the determination of all the guys that we were still going to win.

Wednesday 14 January
Delighted at lunch time, depressed at tea, convinced by the the close that the game should be ours when we finished, needing another 281 runs to win with nine wickets left. It was an exhausting day, certainly one not made to soothe the nerves.

We were badly handicapped which made the task of captaining the side in the field all the harder, trying not to expose our limitations to the Australians. After his opening burst Graham Dilley was forced to go off the field. He had damaged a muscle throwing in a ball from the boundary at the start of the day and his right shoulder stiffened up. He was able to give me only six overs.

During his morning bowling spell Phil Edmonds became a casualty, pulling a groin muscle which limited his movements in the field. He was still able to bowl despite the nagging pain which affected him in his follow-through. Then there was John Emburey. He had insisted on taking the field the evening before the rest day although he could not run. He still could not run today because of his groin strain, and it also affected him in his follow-through. He insisted on doing more than his share of bowling, however, with the pitch taking more turn. Thank goodness he did. It was another courageous performance.

He finished the day with seven for 78, his best return in Test cricket, a true reward for his spirit. At one stage it appeared as though his figures were going to be even better as he threatened to run through the entire Australian side just before lunch. It was a spell which had me thinking in terms of batting again by mid-afternoon.

The breakthrough took a little time in coming as Dean Jones and Allan Border took their overnight partnership to 74 and Australia's total to 106 – a lead of 174 – before we parted them, Border chopping a delivery from Edmonds on to his

*John Emburey who, despite a groin strain, took 7 for 78 in
the second innings of the Sydney Test*

wicket. He had been completely deceived by the turn and attempted to play a square cut. That was the third Australian wicket to fall. By lunch, half an hour later, we had seven down, all of them falling to John in a 49-ball spell that cost him only 16 runs. Jones was taken behind off a very thin edge, Dirk Wellham and Peter Sleep picked up by Allan Lamb at silly point, and Tim Zoehrer leg before, right back in front of his wicket.

Australia were 145 for seven at the break, only 214 runs on with Peter Taylor back at the wicket in another crisis. His partner was Steve Waugh, who should also have been out when he offered a stumping chance to Jack Richards charging down the wicket against Phil.

It turned out to be a crucial error, Jack didn't quite gather the ball cleanly in his eagerness. Waugh was to profit hugely from the escape, and there was another stubborn performance with the bat from Taylor. By tea the two of them were still at the wicket and I had a few strong words to say in the dressing room. I felt we had aided them by not being patient enough. I thought the best way of getting them out, Taylor in particular, was to pile the pressure on them, frustrate them into error, especially when the largish 17,000 crowd began a slow handclap. Instead we attacked too early with both John and Phil bowling a little too straight trying to make Waugh and Taylor play with the bat instead of the pads. It fed them a few safe runs which increased their confidence over the two-hour period.

I was not helped in being without Dilley, who might have made a difference when I took the new ball with the main aim of getting a harder ball for the spinners. I had to turn to Ian Botham to partner Gladstone and Ian is still not bowling off his full run with proper aggression following the rib injury. That six-over interlude also eased the pressure on the batsmen.

At lunch I had been thinking in terms of chasing around 250 with victory still possible. At tea I was staring at an Australian lead of 350, or possibly more, which would have put a victory chase out of the question, survival our only means of escape. I did not want to have to bat too long in those circumstances and decided at tea we must keep it very tight to stop the Australians scoring too quickly.

In the event the Australian innings was soon wrapped up. Waugh surprised us all by suddenly stepping down the wicket and driving a catch to deep mid-on as he tried to hit John over long off, Taylor became a silly point victim and Merv Hughes was bowled having an ungainly heave. Suddenly we were back with 320 to win in just over seven hours, a reasonable target as long as we took it steady and did not lose too many wickets in the evening. We lost only one when Chris Broad drove a return catch to leg spinner Peter Sleep in making 17 runs.

That still gave us a good chance as far as I was concerned and the lads thought the same way. I had suggested to David Gower that he ought to go in at number three if we lost a wicket early because he would be getting more and more trouble outside the off stump from the ball turning in the rough created by the Australian bowlers. Going in early would give David a chance to experience the conditions while the pitch was still relatively clear. He saw the sense in that and agreed.

David Gower scored 68 which helped us to beat the Prime Minister's XI

The Christmas fancy dress party

Chris Broad

Phil DeFreitas

The Fosters with Peter L

James Whitaker and Allan Lamb

Jack and Birgitta Richards

Bill and Janet Athey   David Gower and fiancée Vicky   With Graham Dilley

Mickey Stewart, Laurie Brown with Frances and Phil Edmonds

The colour of one-day cricket in Australia: Ian Botham and Allan Lamb batting during the Perth Challenge and the Grand Slam completed

Border was certainly the captain who looked a little apprehensive this evening when he said to me 'What's going on? It's like playing cricket in India. John Emburey has a runner when he bats but bowls 46 overs taking seven wickets. Graham Dilley goes off when he finishes his spell and is replaced by your best outfield, Daffy. What else is going to happen tomorrow?'

He was obviously a little touchy and I realised then there was no way John would be allowed a runner on the last day, although he is still badly hampered by his injury.

Thursday 15 January

I woke up this morning to newspaper headlines saying that history was against us winning. Only once before had an England side been successful chasing more than 300 to win batting fourth in a Test match, and that had been back in 1928–29 in Melbourne when England made 332 for seven. The newspapers also informed me that there had been only nine other occasions of a side scoring more than 300 to win a Test batting last, the most recent occasion at Lord's in 1984 when Gordon Greenidge had scored a masterly double century for the West Indies.

This did not deter me. I was keen to give it a go in the belief that we would save it if things did not go too wrong. History proved right. It was just beyond us but I felt proud as I left the ground this evening that we had made such a tremendous effort – despite seeing Ian Botham out first ball – failing by only 55 runs. It was very

Ian Botham was out in both innings to the bowling of Taylor

disappointing but we had played our part in making it one of the most fascinating Test matches in which I have played. I only hope it doesn't spoil all the magnificent work we have put in before in regaining the Ashes. It shouldn't. There was no disgrace in losing this game.

Our innings followed a very similar pattern to that of Australia yesterday. A sound start and then the stumble around the lunch period to leave us looking no-hopers at 102 for five – still almost four hours to survive or make 218 to win, it looked impossible.

David and Bill played with considerable care during the first 90 minutes of the day, Bill escaping one chance when Border put down a slip catch when he had made 31. He was still on 31 half an hour later when Border took his first wicket in four years in Test cricket when having David caught at short leg. An over later and Bill perished, deceived in the flight by Sleep and bowled behind his legs attempting to play a sweep shot in his anxiety to get his score moving again. These were both unfortunate ways to go.

The first over after lunch was even worse. That man Taylor again, having Allan Lamb picked up at silly point and Ian chipping to mid-wicket first ball, Wellham taking a good catch. Our position looked impossible yet I still hadn't given up all hope of pulling it off even at that stage. When Jack Richards joined me I stressed the importance of us still being together at tea when we could have another look at the situation. I felt in very good form and I was determined to be positive as long as I stayed at the crease. It was a question of sorting out the good and bad balls. Getting in was sticky. Once in I thought it was possible to stay there as long as you were on your guard, and neither Sleep nor Taylor bowled as tightly as John or Phil. I knew I would get a good ration of poor deliveries to go for boundary shots.

Both of us had our moments. I was a little fortunate when Border brought back Hughes for a short burst. His fourth ball failed to bounce very high and I got an edge Zoehrer failed to hold, the ball only just reaching him. In the next over from Sleep Jack was beaten by the leg break but Border could only knock away the chance as the ball shot towards his face. They were our moments of anxiety although I was becoming increasingly concerned about the way the close in fielders were starting to put pressure on the umpires – Zoehrer in particular.

If the match today was resembling a Test in India then Australia were responsible. Arms were being thrown aloft, appeals shouted every time the ball struck the pad, although I was never sure whether they were asking for a catch or a leg before because there was no way of getting either. I was particularly upset on one occasion when Zoehrer made a great show of appealing for a catch behind against Jack after he had played forward against Sleep and was beaten, the ball missing the bat by some distance. When he made another appeal against me soon afterwards after I had missed an attempted sweep against Taylor, I lost my temper momentarily and had a go at the wicket-keeper, including a couple of choice expletives. I apologised to Border at the end of the over but it worked because he told Zoehrer to calm down.

By tea our victory target was only 133 runs away with an hour and the last 20 overs left. I told Jack it was still on provided we could stay together for that first hour. We did and when the last 20 overs started we were left with another 90 wanted, Australia having taken the new ball half an hour earlier. Again I told Jack that it was still on. It was his turn to say to me: 'We must make sure we get through ten of the last 20 before we really go for it.' I had to agree but thought that if we were going to be able to carry on the way we had been, we would be needing less than 50 at that stage.

Border must have come to the same conclusion because he suddenly turned to Steve Waugh with the idea, I imagine, of trying to slow us down, spreading the field out a little more. Waugh not only slowed us down, he nipped in with a wicket during his second over – mine. I'm not quite sure what happened even now. I attempted to play him through mid wicket and I'm sure I did not play too early. I can only imagine the ball stopped on me, for it hit higher on the bat than I expected and gave the bowler a return catch. I was just four runs short of a second century in the series.

On the way back to the pavilion I stopped long enough on the outfield to tell John Emburey: 'It's still on. Get yourself in and then have a word with Jack to re-assess the situation'. They never did get that chance to re-assess. I haven't had time to talk to John this evening but I have the feeling he didn't think the victory was on after I had been dismissed. He abandoned all hope when Jack misread Sleep's googly and got a thin inside edge to leave us with 63 wanted, 56 balls left and only three wickets in hand. It was survival time now, looking for a draw, and I have to admit I couldn't bear to watch the last few overs as John and Gladstone battled it out, Phil having fallen leg before first ball.

I was given a commentary by the others who told me of Border's deep discussion with almost the whole side before deciding to take Taylor out of the attack and turn to Bruce Reid for the 18th over of the last 20. His fourth ball found the edge of Gladstone's bat and gave Border a slip catch.

There was another huddle, I'm told, at the end of the over before Border decided against asking Hughes to bowl and kept faith with leg spinner Sleep instead. John kept out the first five balls but was forced on to his back foot to deal with the sixth, only find the leg break just evade the edge and bowl him. We had failed to save it by only six balls and I felt very sorry for John that he should have been the last man out after all the brave work he had put in with both the bat and the ball.

Not surprisingly in view of his all-round contribution in the match when returning career best bowling figures and failing by only one run to match his previous best score of 43, Taylor was voted the 'Man of the Match'. Yet the real story of the five match series was told in the award for the 'Man of the Series' which went to Chris Broad for his three centuries in successive Test matches. It demonstrated we had been on top until the very last moment.

I am feeling disappointed this evening but far from down. The Ashes are still with England and I am proud of every member of the side, grateful, too, for their support during the previous three months. I could not have asked for a better spirit, a more determined approach, or more loyal service. Every player in our side has made some contribution at some stage. And that includes the four who did not get into the Tests, yet played such valuable supporting roles.

FIFTH TEST MATCH

Sydney Cricket Ground, January 10, 11, 12, 14, 15

AUSTRALIA		Runs	Mins	Balls	4s		Runs	Mins	Balls	4s
G.R. Marsh	c Gatting b Small	24	87	57	2	(2) c Emburey b Dilley	14	52	39	2
G.M. Ritchie	lbw b Dilley	6	22	12	1	(1) c Botham b Richards	13	67	46	—
D.M. Jones	not out	184	540	420	12*	c Richards b Emburey	30	145	109	2
*A.R.Border	c Botham b Edmonds	34	137	112	3	b Edmonds	49	114	95	8
D.Mc.D. Wellham	c Richards b Small	17	48	48	2	c Lamb b Emburey	1	26	17	—
S.R. Waugh	c Richards b Small	0	1	1	—	c Athey b Emburey	73	185	172	5
P.R. Sleep	c Richards b Small	9	15	15	1	c Lamb b Emburey	10	22	25	2
†T.J. Zoehrer	c Gatting b Small	12	55	38	—	lbw b Emburey	1	11	14	—
P.L. Taylor	c Emburey b Edmonds	11	84	64	1	c Lamb b Emburey	42	160	154	1
M.G. Hughes	c Botham b Edmonds	16	117	108	—	b Emburey	5	30	27	—
B.A. Reid	b Dilley	4	4	3	1	not out	1	6	5	—
Extras	(b12, lb4, w2, nb8)	26				(b5, lb7)	12			
		343	*Plus 1 six				251			

Fall: 8, 58, 149, 184, 184, 200, 232, 271, 338, 343.

Bowling: Dilley 23.5-5-67-2, Small 33-11-75-5, Botham 23-10-42-0, Emburey 30-4-62-0, Edmonds 34-5-79-3, Gatting 1-0-2-0.

Fall: 29, 31, 106, 110, 115, 141, 145, 243, 248, 251.

Bowling: Dilley 15-4-48-1, Small 8-2-17-0, Edmonds 43-16-79-2, Emburey 46-15-78-7, Botham 3-0-17-0, Gatting 2-2-0-0.

ENGLAND		Runs	Mins	Balls	4s		Runs	Mins	Balls	4s
B.C. Broad	lbw b Hughes	6	22	18	1	c&b Sleep	17	38	31	1
C.W.J. Athey	c Zoehrer b Hughes	5	12	7	1	b Sleep	31	164	134	3
*M.W. Gatting	lbw b Reid	0	4	2	—	(5) c&b Waugh	96	210	161	10 *
A.J. Lamb	c Zoehrer b Taylor	24	91	60	4	c Waugh b Taylor	3	45	25	—
D.I.Gower	c Wellham b Taylor	72	142	114	12	(3) c Marsh b Border	37	119	92	5
I.T. Botham	c Marsh b Taylor	16	15	13	2*	c Wellham b Taylor	0	1	1	—
†C.J. Richards	c Wellham b Reid	46	165	136	7	b Sleep	38	217	165	2
J.E. Emburey	b Taylor	69	210	168	8	b Sleep	22	67	56	4
P.H. Edmonds	c Marsh b Taylor	3	14	14	—	lbw b Sleep	0	1	1	—
G.C. Small	b Taylor	14	54	31	1	c Border b Reid	0	26	19	—
G.R. Dilley	not out	4	9	4	1	not out	2	5	2	—
Extras	(b9, lb3, w2, nb2)	16				(b8, lb6, w1, nb3)	18			
		275	*Plus 1 six				264	*Plus 1 six		

Fall: 16, 17, 17, 89, 119, 142, 213, 219, 270, 275.

Bowling: Hughes 16-3-58-2, Reid 25-7-74-2, Waugh 6-4-6-0, Taylor 26-7-78-6, Sleep 21-6-47-0.

Fall: 24, 91, 91, 102, 102, 233, 257, 257, 262, 264.

Bowling: Hughes 12-3-32-0, Reid 19-8-32-1, Sleep 35-14-72-5, Taylor 29-10-76-2, Border 13-6-25-1, Waugh 6-2-13-1.

Toss won by Australia
Man of the Match: P.L. Taylor
Man of the Series: B.C. Broad

Test debuts: P.L. Taylor (Aus)
Umpires: P.J. McConnell & S.G. Randell

AUSTRALIA WON BY 55 RUNS

World Series challenge — first leg

Friday 16 January

Another dawn patrol. There is just no time to sit back and relax, and take in the finish of the Test series. Up at 7 am, bags down in the hotel by 7.45, off to the airport for a 9.30 flight to Brisbane in readiness for tomorrow's start of the World Series one-day competition when we take on the West Indies. Somebody has worked out that this was our 29th take-off on the tour and there are still a few more to go yet before touching down at Heathrow. It is beginning to seem as though we have been here forever, our first sight of Brisbane back in October something of the distant past.

Brisbane was in the middle of one of those sticky weather periods when storms threaten but never arrive to clear the atmosphere. It had been over 100°F yesterday, was just under 100°F when we arrived and the forecast was for another sweltering day tomorrow with humidity around 70 per cent. It was no place to be walking about. Bed was most appealing this afternoon – a chance to catch up on sleep before the team meeting.

We will be without Phil Edmonds tomorrow. His groin strain had not eased and he cannot run. Fortunately John is much better and Graham Dilley has recovered from his shoulder strain. We decided to make just one change from the Test side with DeFreitas taking over from Edmonds. The West Indies are at full strength and there is no question we would catch them cold this time. While we had been in Sydney, they had been in Townsville, Queensland, playing a one-day match and a three-day match against the full state side. They had lost the one-day game after failing to make 200 and Viv Richards arrived in Brisbane with his team this afternoon making threatening noises to them about improving their record.

Saturday 17 January

Another victory over the West Indies, the first time, I gather, that England have beaten them in successive one-day internationals. It was won for us by our bowlers and I don't think I have ever seen such outstanding bowling by all five concerned in one game. Not one no-ball. Not one wide. Apart from one mishap, the fielding was high class, too. They were shot out for 154 in 46.3 overs, and when they failed to make a breakthrough with their fast bowlers, Viv virtually gave up.

We were helped by me winning the toss; I put them in on a pitch which encouraged the pace bowlers, but it was still tough work in the most oppressive conditions I have ever experienced. The temperature soared to just over 100°F in the shade and I'd hate to guess what it was out in the middle. There was no wind either. Just walking around the fielding left everybody dripping, chasing after the ball made us gasp for breath.

After six of his ten overs Gladstone Small was forced to go off with heat exhaustion and needed ice-pack treatment in the dressing room to cool down. By the end of the West Indies innings Graham Dilley was almost out on his feet and needed a long time to recover. Even the West Indians found the going extremely hard, and once Viv had made up his mind there was no chance of bowling us out, he never bothered to turn to Marshall, Holding or Garner again and spared them a further fast bowling ordeal in the heat.

Dilley was our most successful fast bowler and I felt we had the measure of the West Indies after his sixth over when he had Richie Richardson edging to slip and then bowled Viv Richards via an inside edge. With DeFreitas having trapped Gordon Greenidge leg before in his first over, the West Indies were 26 for three and 11 overs gone. They were rescued by Desmond Haynes and Gus Logie who added 86 together in 21 overs before both showed the type of indisciplined approach the West Indies were noted for before Clive Lloyd turned them into such a ruthless and professional side. One of them needed to stay there if the West Indies were going to make a decent score, but both were out to catches in the deep mid-wicket area heaving across the line in successive overs from John Emburey. After that, it was all over.

We had one mishap fairly early on when Bill Athey was caught behind against Holding, but once David Gower started stroking the ball around without too much difficulty, supported by Chris Broad, Viv threw in the towel and the rest of us were able to canter home with almost six overs to spare.

All of us were too exhausted afterwards to show that much delight in beating the West Indies once again, but it was very satisfying.

England v West Indies
Played at Brisbane, Jan 17

West Indies 154 (46.3 overs)
England 156 for 4 (44.1 overs)

England won by 6 wickets.   Man of Match: G. Dilley

Sunday 18 January

We paid the price today for our exertions in yesterday's heat. We were defeated by the Australians when we fell 12 runs short chasing a 262-run victory target. A great pity really, for we still should have won.

Allan Border said afterwards that our tiredness was one reason why he decided to bat first, hoping to chip a few extra runs out of us, counting on our reactions not being as slick as usual. They were not. The bowling wasn't so precise either. There was a little zip missing from Graham Dilley, while Gladstone Small's line was not as immaculate as usual. Seven days cricket in nine days – one of the non-playing days, a tiring travelling day – each one involving a high degree of tension, had taken its toll on the faster bowlers. Phil DeFreitas was the pick today but he had not played in the Sydney Test.

Chip extra runs Australia did, especially over the first half of their innings. It was that man Dean Jones again, who made another century against us, his third in successive matches. It was also his third century in four one-day games, having made two in Perth. He was backed this time by Geoff Marsh playing with greater freedom than ever before, the two teaming up when Dirk Wellham – Australia's latest opener – was out with the score on 48.

Australia reached 194 at the end of the 40th over, with Wellham our only success, and I feared we would be chasing somewhere around the 300 mark if they really gave it the gun over the last quarter of their innings. Instead we restricted them well. The lads roused themselves, although the heat was almost as bad as yesterday. Fortunately the humidity level was down and there was a slight breeze.

We were helped by John Emburey bowling Jones the ball after he reached his century, and the fact that Marsh slowed down as he approached his own hundred. He never did reach it, Dilley returned with a better last four overs to dismiss him and Border.

I thought we should have been capable of beating Australia with a bit to spare. We matched the Australians scoring rate when at its fastest, our 150 coming up in the 36th over, only five balls slower than theirs. Unfortunately we also started losing wickets, our fatigue showing in our choice of shots. David Gower was so upset when he was bowled middle stump that he even took a whack at the wicket, completely out of character for a man who usually takes his disappointments so well.

Bill Athey was the only one who stayed around and we really needed him to be there at the end as he had done at Old Trafford last summer against New Zealand when he made an unbeaten 142. Unfortunately he couldn't make the distance. Bill is a very correct player, and the Australians also frustrated him well with their field placings so that many of his best strokes brought no result.

He was also getting very tired, he'd been on the field from the start of the match, and got out when we still needed another 37. There were four overs remaining but we had only two wickets left. John Emburey made another brave effort, suddenly crashing three fours off successive balls against Steve Waugh in the 49th over but 19 runs off the final over bowled by Bruce Reid was just too much. We managed seven to lose by 11 runs.

I sounded off this evening a little about the tour schedule. We had certainly had the worst of it this weekend playing two games back to back. The West Indies had had the benefit of two completely free days before playing us on Saturday and

Australia had had two days in which to recover from the Test match. They also had the benefit of three new faces in Simon O'Donnell, Greg Matthews and Ken MacLeay who had all been playing cricket regularly. We had talked about making changes just to give a couple of players a rest but decided it was unfair to ask James Whitaker to bat or Neil Foster to bowl, neither having played since Tasmania. I suppose we are now victims of our own success in fielding a regular and settled side.

It was not sour grapes about the defeat. I had raised doubts about the working schedule before setting off from Heathrow. It had looked tough on paper. It was even tougher in actuality, far more demanding than I thought. The Test and County Cricket Board had managed to get the qualifying matches for the World Series cut down from ten each to eight in view of the extra competition in Perth. I thought they should have been reduced to six each in order to allow more recovery time. The cricket authorities must be careful not to overtax players otherwise they will be in danger of creating boredom for the players and public alike.

England v Australia
Played at Brisbane, Jan 18

Australia 261 for 4 (50 overs) (G.R. Marsh 93, D.M. Jones 101)
England 250 for 9 (50 overs) (C.W.J. Athey 111)

Australia won by 11 runs.   Man of Match: D.M. Jones

Monday 19 January

We decided last night that the lads had had enough of cricket for the time being. Our next match is not until Thursday in Sydney, they are all in form with only physical exhaustion causing problems yesterday, so three days away was the order. This was helped by the fact that manager Peter Lush had booked us into a block of new apartments at Bondi Junction. There were no bars, no public places for people to gather, and this helped the peaceful feeling.

Although cricket was off the menu I still felt the need to keep fit and I went for a run this evening along the cliffs between Bondi and Coogee beaches. The views are lovely. This evening was another chance to relax with a change of scenery out with the Carney family. Don Carney had been doctor to the New South Wales side during my time with Balmain until he had died two years ago. His widow Barbara and the rest of the family made me feel welcome.

Tuesday 20 January

Another lazy day, although I went for a run this morning and attended a book signing session this afternoon. I was promoting my book on limited-over cricket – too late for the Australian team to take advantage I hope!

This evening I put my feet up in the apartment and watched the West Indies beat Australia by seven wickets with 10 balls to spare in Melbourne; a good result for us, all three teams are level on points at the quarter stage of the qualifying rounds.

The Australians had been in trouble at 74 for five – including Dirk Wellham and Greg Matthews who had been run out – after 31 overs. Once again Allan Border came to their rescue, this time with the help of Simon O'Donnell. They put on 91 for the sixth wicket in 17 overs; O'Donnell suddenly went on the rampage after taking a while to get his eye in. His 52 came off 64 balls and helped boost Australia to 181 for six, Michael Holding having been responsible for slowing them down in conceding only 15 runs from his 10 overs.

It was never enough to challenge the West Indies, although they might have been in trouble if the Australians had managed a quick breakthrough, for Viv Richards had not wanted to bat after damaging his left hand in fielding practice. He was never required as Desmond Haynes and little Gus Logie made sure of a West Indies win. They never had to hurry.

Wednesday 21 January

Many of the side spent yesterday sailing through Sydney Harbour on the yacht *Condor*, which had recently returned from taking part in the Sydney to Hobart race. There is never a shortage of invitations in Australia.

Today was booked for shopping for most of the team. If we run into trouble in the World Series Cup, this could be our last free day in Sydney on the tour. We had to take advantage of it. I went into the city for another book signing session and ended the day at a dinner thrown by the Western Suburb League Club who raised a lot of money for the Wests Club. It was a nice way to finish off a very handy three-day break. Back to business under the floodlights at Sydney tomorrow and I hope the others feel as rested as I do.

Thursday 22 January

Astonishing, absolutely astonishing. There must be something about Sydney, us and dramatic finishes. There could not have been many in the history of the World Series Cup to match this one when Allan Lamb faced up to the final over from Bruce Reid with us needing 18 runs to win. He got them with one ball to spare to give us a three-wicket win over Australia and put us back at the top of the qualifying table.

I must admit I thought we had lost it, although with Lambie facing anything is always possible. I knew he would have a go but I had my doubts because he had struggled through most of his innings, seldom managing to time his strokes. It wasn't until afterwards that I learned he had faced 97 balls for his 59 runs when the last over started and had not managed to hit one boundary. Now we needed at least a couple. It was no trouble in the end as Lambie hit 2, 4, 6, 2 and 4 off the first five balls; the six was the turning point as it sailed magnificently over wide mid-wicket and finished about 10 rows deep into the terracing. He had a little luck with

Allan Lamb batting during the World Series Cup. He scored 18 runs off the last over with one ball to spare to win the game for England and the Man of Match award for himself

his next stroke, struck firmly to extra cover. There was only a single in it which would have left Daffy DeFreitas on strike, having only recently arrived at the crease. The luck was in Reid not taking the return cleanly – he was unsighted – which enabled Lambie to take a second, keep the strike and hit the next ball for four.

His efforts gave him the 'Man of the Match' award, which had been lined up for Dirk Wellham at the start of the last over following his 97 – his highest one-day score. It had formed the backbone of Australia's 233 for eight after Allan Border had won the toss. That was a little higher than I wanted to chase but considerably less than it might have been after Wellham and Geoff Marsh had put on 109 together inside the first 26 overs. We had needed our three-day break but we looked a little rusty in the field for the first half of the Australian innings, although we had practised this morning. We were not moving sharply enough and the pair of them were able to get far too many twos when we should have limited them to singles, and put pressure on them.

Once we made the breakthrough when Marsh was caught behind off Phil Edmonds, we were able to re-establish our grip aided by some marvellous catching by Bill Athey in the short mid-wicket position. Two of his three to take Dean Jones and Steve Waugh were classic efforts. Graham Dilley chipped in with another at long off to dismiss Border, and Australia made only 43 runs off their last ten overs losing five wickets. That gave us the chance, an opportunity I thought we must not miss a second time after we had lost out in Brisbane when we had slowed the Australians up to leave us with a manageable target. It wasn't going to be easy. The Australians had shown that they had learned from their errors in Perth. They were getting more fielders in the right positions and Border was making a better selection of bowlers for certain situations.

Bill Athey, for instance, had trouble making two off 22 deliveries before he was out. At one stage in his innings, Allan Lamb was restricted to 25 successive singles moving from three to 28. Fortunately Chris Broad was in a confident mood and made his 45 off only 58 balls and David Gower played very sensibly. When he was out and I was bowled for only one, we slipped a little but victory still looked on when we started the last ten overs needing 73 with six wickets left. It was when Ian Botham was out for a breezy 27 that we started to slip. John Emburey and Jack

---

England v Australia
Played at Sydney, Jan 22

Australia 233 for 8 (50 overs) (D. Wellham 97)
England 234 for 7 (49.5 overs) (A.J. Lamb 71*, D.I. Gower 50)

England won by 3 wickets.   Man of Match: A.J. Lamb

Richards soon followed and the going got tough when our asking rate rose to over ten an over with three overs remaining, two from Reid and one from Steve Waugh who was bowling tightly.

Normally I shy away from watching at this stage but I studied every ball of Allan's thrilling finale which had the whole dressing room jumping up in the air with delight. It was a vital victory. There would have been a danger of us falling apart a little if we had lost to Australia again. Now we were on course for the finals, back in the mood for the Adelaide Australia Day weekend.

Friday 23 January

I couldn't help but notice a headline in a Sydney newspaper this morning as we prepared to fly to Adelaide. 'Australia Filthy over Lamb' it said. Underneath was a story suggesting that Australian players were unhappy about Allan Lamb getting in the way from the return from extra cover last night which Bruce Reid fumbled, allowing Allan to go for a second, keep the strike and hit the victory four. The story said some Australian players were suggesting Allan had deliberately blocked Reid's view causing him to fumble. No Australian players were named, of course. There was a quote from team manager Bobby Simpson saying they were not making a complaint. What utter rubbish! I think it must have been Australian newspaper reaction to yet another shock defeat. It failed to point out that Allan and the ball arrived at the crease at the same time and there was no suggestion in the television replays that Allan was looking at the thrower, he was just concentrating on making his ground. I wonder what they will think of next.

Our only problem for the West Indies match tomorrow concerns Phil Edmonds who is feeling the groin strain he suffered during the last Test match. In the end we settled for making Phil 12th man at tonight's selection meeting and recalling Gladstone Small. With the short boundaries square on either side of the wicket at Adelaide, we decided playing two spinners against the West Indies was a bit of a gamble.

Saturday 24 January

They have a television competition over here showing the 'Classic Catches' of the summer, which the winner has to put in correct order. Every one of the ten or 12 catches they will show at the end of the season should be taken from England examples. I would have to be the sole judge of the best, but the one Chris Broad took today would have to be in the frame.

It was a superb, athletic effort at long on which cut off the power of Viv Richards just when he was beginning to threaten our command of the match. With Viv gone victory was ours – a third one-day win in a row against the West Indies, something no other country has ever managed since one-day internationals started. What a first.

Chris Broad and Bill Athey both scored half centuries in putting down a 121-run start inside the first 32 overs, and we finished up with 252 for six. We were boosted by Allan Lamb and John Emburey carving 33 off the last three overs which

Malcolm Marshall and Courtney Walsh bowled off a few paces so the West Indies could get through their 50 overs inside the allotted time and escaped a fine.

I thought it would be enough with the way we had been bowling in the competition. Phil DeFreitas made sure it was with an inspired opening burst that removed Gordon Greenidge and Richie Richardson – although he might have been a little lucky with the Greenidge leg before. But he deserved it anyway.

Our one concern left was Viv. Twenty overs of him in full flight can make any score look stupid. He hadn't achieved much in Australia so far but it doesn't take long to light his fire. He got a start this time, gradually found a little of his touch and began to strike out as his confidence returned. He had already hit one six over

Bill Athey who, along with Chris Broad, helped England to a fine start against the West Indies

long on, which is a fair carry on this Adelaide ground, when he went for another against Ian Botham. Chris was out there in the distance but, from my viewpoint, I never thought he and the ball would ever come together. It looked out of his reach, which was Chris's first reaction. Fortunately he kept going, stretched out his right hand and the ball stuck as he was in full stride.

It was a wonderful effort. Certainly Chris liked it, the way he ran around the boundary edge, his right arm punching the air. The rest of us certainly did. Viv's dismissal left the West Indies on 92 for four, his 43 runs having been scored from 72 added whilst he was at the wicket. Without him the rest folded against John Emburey's off spin, aided by more fine catching. It left us winners by 89 runs with 4.1 overs left, a comprehensive victory. The West Indies had been outplayed. It was no fluke. We were word perfect again as we had been in the Perth competition. Elton had returned to us after sampling the Australian Open Tennis Championships and it was a very nice way to welcome him back. With a day off before tackling the Australians again, we had time to celebrate this victory, too.

England v West Indies
Played at Adelaide Jan 24

England 252 for 6 (50 overs) (C.W.J. Athey 64, B.C. Broad 55)
West Indies 163 (45.5 overs)

England won by 89 runs.   Man of Match: B.C. Broad

Sunday 25 January

There were a number of worrying signs about the West Indies today as they bounced back to beat the Australians by 16 runs, a margin which sounds closer than it actually was. They had a 90-minute meeting behind locked dressing-room doors last night after our victory and I understand there were some pretty frank exchanges. They appear to have had the desired effect, aided by Viv showing more evidence for the second successive day that his touch is returning.

He was the second highest West Indian scorer, making 69 off 64 balls with two sixes and seven fours. They had another bonus in Richie Richardson showing his first sign of form on the tour, making 72 towards their 237 for five standing in as opener for the injured Gordon Greenidge. Perhaps the most significant contribution was the 42 made by the left-handed Larry Gomes, a former Middlesex colleague, who had been declared fit after a shoulder injury. I feel he is the essential middle-order link-pin in the West Indies side. He is a sobering influence who does not deal in boundaries, but keeps his head, works the gaps and provides their innings with a backbone built on smartly taken ones and twos. Without him they are flashy and suspect. With him they are a unit, he is a batsman who complements the strokeplay of the others and makes their batting work.

There was one other difference between the West Indies of today and the side we played 24 hours earlier. Their fast bowlers were sharper, the result, so I have been told, of a taunt thrown at them by manager Steve Camacho who wanted to know how Phil DeFreitas had managed to look sharper, hit the ground harder and appeared more menacing than the famous West Indian pace attack. The taunt hit home.

Not that most of us were bothered by Australia's 16 run defeat, Australia's answer was built around Geoff Marsh's 94. A courageous effort for a player who is never really going to take any attack apart.

Most of us visited a vineyard today, sampling some of South Australia's finest wines. In strict moderation of course.

Monday 26 January

My mood of elation after Saturday's victory over the West Indies turned into one of deep depression this evening after we had thrown away another victory against Australia by the type of frantic batting I thought we had put behind us. We should never have lost and there is a doubt now about us making the World Series Cup finals and completing an Australian grand slam.

Everything had gone so smoothly at the start. Inside the first 12 overs we had reduced Australia to 37 for three, bringing Steve Waugh in to join Allan Border. That was the start of things going wrong. He was 29 when Border slogged merrily at Ian Botham only to sky the ball to deep mid on where Graham Dilley was stationed. It looked a comfortable catch but Graham lost it in the sun – and spilled the chance.

We had one other chance of getting rid of Border when he had made 51. He was sent back by Waugh attempting a smart single. He was well out of his ground when the ball was returned to Ian but his shy at the stumps from six feet missed. Border and Waugh went on to add 164 for the fourth wicket – a record for the competition – yet we still managed to limit them to 225 for six. It was well within our reach on the pure Adelaide pitch.

I thought we had it in the bag by the time we reached the last 20 overs of our innings. We needed just over 100 to win with eight wickets in hand, leaving us an asking rate of five an over. With sensible batting it should have been all over, another two points pocketed, our fourth win behind us and virtually certain of a place in the finals. Instead we blew it in a big way, losing our last eight batsmen for 67 runs and finishing 33 runs short. I had to give some credit to the Australian bowlers, however, especially as they were without Bruce Reid who had a groin strain. That should have made our task easier for he is still their most effective one-day bowler, despite that 18 Allan Lamb took off him in Sydney.

I had decided to revert to the number four position for this game. Earlier I had noticed that Allan Lamb had struggled to assert himself when he went in around the 20-over stage, finding himself up against either off spinners Peter Taylor or Greg Matthews. In Sydney I had pushed Ian Botham up the order against Australia in order to give him more chance of playing himself in before opening up. That move had not come off. This time I thought it would be better if *I* took on the spinners in the middle of the innings.

The move appeared to work when I joined Chris Broad after Bill Athey and David Gower had fallen. Together, Chris and I put on 70 for the third wicket and kept the score ticking along at around four an over, with the asking rate being 4.5. Then came the 32nd over, and things started to go wrong.

I was hoping Chris would be able to stay there and keep one end going, but he

suddenly went for a big hit over the top only to find Border at deep mid off instead. It provided Steve Waugh with a breakthrough. Three overs later I had also fallen and, looking back, I should have been less impetuous. Following Chris's dismissal things had gone a little quiet, with Allan finding the fielders with his shots just as he had done at Sydney. Two overs had produced two runs so when Taylor came on I tried to get us moving again. It was a mistake.

Taylor tossed one up a little which I thought I could hit safely inside out over extra cover. I took a couple of steps down the wicket, missed and was bowled. The floodgates were opened. That was followed by a horrible mix-up between Ian and Allan which resulted in Allan being run out when sent back going for a quick single. During the various calamities to follow the asking rate rose steeply. It became too much for the others, forced to hit out as soon as they arrived at the crease. We were bowled out with 11 balls still to spare.

The player I felt most sorry for was Phil DeFreitas who opened up with an astonishing first seven overs, capturing the wickets of Geoff Marsh, Dirk Welham and Dean Jones for 17 runs. He was fast, hostile and obtained surprising bounce from a wicket three days old. Marsh fell to another superb diving catch by John Emburey in the gully, the other two to catches behind when surprised by the bounce. He might easily have had a fourth in that spell when Waugh got an edge first ball, fending off a rising delivery. Botham spilled the catch at slip but, fortunately for him, square-leg umpire Tony Crafter had ruled no-ball on the grounds that the ball went through above shoulder height.

It was 'Man of the Match' stuff from Daffy, especially when he added a fourth wicket on his return having Border caught for 91. We spoiled his chances of collecting the award by our batting. Altogether it was a depressing performance, and Micky Stewart came out with some strong words on our return to the dressing room, shouting against the strains of 'Waltzing Matilda' being played at full blast on the ground's tannoy system. It was Australia Day – and we had made the day for them. I'm not in a talkative mood this evening as most people have noticed.

England v Australia
Played at Adelaide, Jan 26

Australia 225 for 6 (50 overs) (A.R. Border 91, S.R. Waugh 83*)
England 192 (49.1 overs)

Australia won by 33 runs.   Man of Match: S.W. Waugh

Matthews kneels in despair, as England battle on for victory

The Grand Slam!

Tuesday 27 January

Reading the Australian newspapers this morning I was disappointed with the way they had painted us as a cocky side in yesterday's game based on a remark Allan Border made at the end of match press conference. I hope Allan didn't say it in the way it was reported and would like to think it was taken out of context.

The reports gave the impression that we had all indulged in a lot of sniping during the Border-Steve Waugh partnership, taking the whole thing too lightly, and making constant snide references about Australia's attack, saying it was nothing without the injured Bruce Reid and we could easily top whatever runs they made. The reports took great delight in knocking us down. A couple of such remarks were made out in the middle to Allan but by only one man – Ian Botham. Then again Ian has a special relationship with Allan, with whom he will be playing for Queensland from now on. It was his idea of a bit of gamesmanship which I thought was a little dangerous and did ask him to stop. To suggest we had all been at it was quite false and it did not help my mood. I was still annoyed at letting the match get away from us.

Wednesday 28 January

Our task of reaching the finals began to look harder this evening as we flew into Melbourne from Adelaide in readiness for our next two qualifying rounds. We arrived in time to catch the last hour of the Australia-West Indies match in Sydney on television – in time to see Australia reverse the trend in games between the two countries and come out on top. They were getting their act together at last.

They were helped by playing the game again on that rolled strip of mud which had been used for our match a few days earlier. It suited the spin and medium-pace attack of Australia better than the West Indies fast men. It was a poor pitch for a one-day game and Viv Richards could not have been very pleased.

For a while he looked as though he might win it for his side after Australia had been bowled out for 194 in exactly 50 overs, four of their last five batsmen being run out. With the West Indies making a poor start it soon became Viv against the rest and he could have done it if he had found one person to stay with him. He made 70 off 96 balls but the batsmen at the other end became too excitable, getting out to rash strokes and the West Indies went down by 33 runs.

That did not help our cause. Each time we had beaten the West Indies, they had roused themselves and scored an overwhelming victory in their next game over Australia. Now their next game was against us in two days' time! It set me wondering.

Thursday 29 January

Physiotherapist Laurie Brown is fast becoming a key figure in our party as the heavy schedule starts to produce all sorts of aches and strains. The queue outside his door for treatment is getting longer each morning with Chris Broad's hamstring strain and Graham Dilley's shoulder problem the more serious. Most of the players are now having problems with throwing – only John Emburey, Phil DeFreitas and myself of the side that played in the last game are still able to throw properly. Working out fielding positions is becoming a difficulty. We are all starting to feel very drained, almost reaching the stage where getting out of bed to face another day's play is becoming an unthinkable act – especially the time we have to get out of bed to play these games.

I just can't see why they have to start at 10 am outside Queensland, the only state where they have trouble with the light. In Sydney, Adelaide and Melbourne it doesn't start getting dark until well after 7.30 pm and I see no reason why the matches should have to start before 10.45 at the earliest – except that it might interfere with the programme schedules of Channel Nine who have the television rights. It is a pity that television seems able to dictate to cricket in Australia, instead of it being the other way around.

A 10 am start means leaving the hotel shortly after eight in order to get everything done – such as study the wicket, make the final decision over the team and get in a little knock and fielding practice. Once that is over most players like to sit down quietly for 15 minutes or so to relax and prepare themselves mentally. A 10 am start means everything is done at a rush, which is not the best way to prepare. Perhaps it is something else the Australian Cricket Board should consider along with a reduction of qualifying matches when they renew their television contract in 1989.

Friday 30 January

As I feared the West Indies came gunning for us today and we were beaten by six wickets. It was not a very illustrious performance although the batting conditions were always difficult. We were bowled out for only 147 runs, but the West Indies took 48.2 overs to get home safely, despite the fact that their run rate is poor and they need to improve it rapidly. It could make the difference between making the final and going out if they find themselves level on points with ourselves or Australia at the end.

We had one setback before the start when Graham Dilley, after coming through a test, announced himself fit to bowl, only to throw his arm out again during a short fielding practice session. It did give us a chance of bringing Neil Foster into the game and he bowled beautifully, adding an extra zip to our fielding as well, which eased my problems a little. It gave me an extra man to field in the deep who was able to get the ball back quickly and accurately. That still left me with six who could not.

I did not help our cause when I read the pitch conditions wrongly in deciding to bat first and we never really competed against the full West Indies attack. Some media men had started to write off the West Indies side, suggesting they were over the hill and were about to crack up. They would not have written that if they had been in the middle.

Chris Broad stuck around bravely in trying to keep one end intact but the rest of us failed to support him. We were not helped when Allan Lamb was run out for the second match in succession, further evidence that the length of the tour is getting to us, affecting our judgement. We all knew what we had to do but were not quite as sharp or alert as we should have been in trying to do it. It was left to John Emburey to add some respectability to our innings with a top score of 34, but our miserly 147 was never going to be enough to defend unless something startling happened.

It did not. Viv made sure of that. He dictated the pace of the West Indies reply, fully content to take up the whole distance if necessary in treating our attack with the greatest respect. When the asking rate rose to above four an over, he simply hit John Emburey for a six on two occasions with mighty blows to put his side on course again. It's now getting tight in the qualifying race. We still need one more victory with two matches to go.

England v West Indies
Played at Melbourne, Jan 30

England 147 (50 overs)
West Indies 148 for 4 (48.2 overs) (I.V.A. Richards 58)

West Indies won by 6 wickets.   Man of Match: I.V.A. Richards

---

Saturday 31 January

Our situation demanded a rethink today ready for our match against Australia in Melbourne tomorrow; we decided it was time to try something new. Our main concern was getting the best out of Ian as a batsman. We had shuffled him up and down the order from four to six without obtaining any real benefit and we suggested to him today that he should open against Australia. He has done it before in one-day internationals and Ian's response was typical. He said he would do whatever we thought best for the side.

It had two benefits from our point of view. It gave Ian the chance to bat a little longer, instead of coming in when there were 20 or less overs to go. He could also take advantage of the playing conditions that require nine players inside the circle for the first 15 overs. This would give us a faster start than we had been getting previously. Our original intention was to ask Bill Athey to go in at number three but David Gower said he still preferred that position so we let him have his way and stay there.

Our second change was to leave out Jack Richards whose batting had gone off in the last four or five matches under the strain of playing virtually non-stop for the last two months. He had also had a touch of 'flu which had left him a little lethargic and jaded. It was nice to be able to give Bruce French a chance after the bad luck that had dogged him all tour. We felt that a couple of fresh faces combined with a new outlook would do the trick and put us back on course. We felt confident we could still make it.

Sunday 1 February

Dean Jones is becoming a real menace these days although I have to admit we have contributed to his success by dropping sharp chances he offered on his way to two of his centuries against us.

Today his failed to reach three figures but was only seven runs short in helping the Australians to their 248 for 5 – a chanceless innings this time although I thought I had got rid of him when he had made only 45. Bruce French made a marvellous stumping attempt off my bowling as Jones stretched forward to play an out-swinging delivery but he got his back foot in the crease just in time. It was disappointing because we badly needed a wicket to pull us together. For the first time in the series, our bowling attack was off line and our batting was even worse.

The experiment in opening with Ian came off – he finished our top scorer with 45, but none of the rest of us could make any headway against an Australian side gaining in confidence. We were all out for 139, the saddest return of the one-day series and beaten by a handsome 109 runs.

That was enough to guarantee Australia a place in the finals after they had looked the outsiders only three weeks ago. Instead we were looking to be the outsiders with one match to play against the West Indies which we needed to win to stand a chance. They had two games left. We were a very subdued bunch this evening.

England v Australia
Played at Melbourne, Feb 1

Australia 248 for 5 (50 overs) (D.M. Jones 93)
England 139 (47.3 overs)
Australia won by 109 runs.   Man of Match: S.R. Waugh

Monday 2 February

The full extent of our failure yesterday came home today as we prepared to move to Davenport on the northern Tasmania coast for our final qualifying match. At the same time Peter Lush was forced to prepare the groundwork for us returning home a week ahead of schedule. The Australian Board would cut off the tour expenses for the side which failed to reach the finals as soon as the qualifying rounds were over.

There were also alternative flight arrangements to be made in addition to alternative hotel accommodation. If we win tomorrow we return to Melbourne for the finals. If we lose we go to Sydney instead as the first stage toward leaving Australia next Saturday. It was a strange feeling and I could even sense the feeling of disappointment of those people at home who had been willing us to take the Australian grand slam.

The other players were feeling distressed as well as we made our way to Melbourne airport. By this evening, however, after a very good team meeting, the mood changed and I went to bed with a feeling we could still pull it off, even though it meant beating the West Indies for a fourth time in five matches. The only sad note was concern about Wilf Slack who collapsed in the nets this afternoon. He was rushed to hospital for tests, but the word from Micky Stewart is that Wilf is feeling okay.

Tuesday 3 February

We are in the final – barring a West Indian miracle – after another astonishing day, spearheaded by Chris Broad with the bat and our bowlers who performed with such control that the West Indies were bowled out for only 148 chasing our 177 total. A day when everything worked to perfection in the field even though the scorecard of our innings made sorry reading for most of us.

That mood of confidence I sensed last night was still with us this morning, especially when Gladstone Small reported fit from a stomach upset. We had made efforts to find the whereabouts of Kent's Richard Ellison in case we needed to call him into the side as Graham Dilley was still unfit, but Gladstone's smile over breakfast assured us everything was okay with him.

Perhaps what really got us going was Ian Botham in the dressing room saying 'You don't want to go home yet because it's too cold back there. Why not make sure of staying an extra week and winning the thing?' Ian had really got worked up about finishing the tour on a high note in order to say farewell to playing for his country overseas.

That was a bonus and so was the fact that Desmond Haynes had dislocated a finger in fielding practice yesterday and reported this morning that it was still too sore for him to hold a bat. The West Indians pleaded with Gordon Greenidge to have a go despite his hamstring strain, but he said it was too bad. Michael Holding was also missing – he had badly strained a hamstring when he took a spectacular return catch to dismiss Ian in our last match. They were therefore without three of their most experienced players.

Not that it made much difference when Viv won the toss, put us in and then unleashed the fast bowlers he did have left to make us struggle. Chris was absolutely superb again, strong and defiant even though he was struggling with his hamstring problem. He even thought of asking for a runner towards the end of his innings but decided against it, believing it would cause too much confusion when attempting quick singles. It was a brave performance, 73 wonderful runs with only Allan Lamb of the other recognised batsmen reaching double figures in making 36.

A total of 177 did not appear large enough even taking into consideration the weakened West Indies batting, but I thought it gave us a good chance if we could bowl properly on a pitch offering uneven bounce. I could not have asked for better support.

The West Indies never got into a challenging position and when Viv – who had dropped himself down to number five for some strange reason – was bowled for just one attempting to cut Ian, I knew we had them. Having failed with the bat, Ian was determined to make up for it with the ball and chipped in with three wickets. His was the best return, but the other four bowlers performed equally heroically and every catch was taken. It was not until afterwards that I realised that five of the six bowling changes I made resulted in a wicket falling immediately. Our pre-match planning with Micky had come off – we got the field set properly for each batsmen.

Mathematically the West Indies still had a chance of pipping us, as long as they won their final qualifying match in Sydney. Not only had they to win, however, they needed to bat first and score 373 runs from 50 overs to beat our scoring rate. It was never going to be on and Viv virtually conceded defeat this evening when he shook my hand and wished me luck in the finals.

England v West Indies
Played at Devonport, Feb 3

England 177 for 9 (50 overs) (B.C. Broad 76)
West Indies 148 (48 overs)

England won by 29 runs.   Man of Match: B.C. Broad

Final Qualifying Table

	P	W	L	Pts
Australia	8	5	3	10
England	8	4	4	8
West Indies	8	3	5	6

Wednesday 4 February

Now that the final is settled I couldn't help wondering about the venues for the qualifying rounds. The Devonport pitch was the fastest we had encountered, made more complicated by the unpredictable bounce. The match also took place on a bitterly cold day with a fierce wind forcing the umpires to wear coats. It was also the first one-day international the ground had staged.

Bearing the last point in mind I would have thought it more fitting if Australia had visited Devonport to launch the ground's international life. Instead we found ourselves taking on the world's most lethal attack there while the Australians were booked to meet the West Indies twice on the slow turning Sydney pitch. Perhaps I'm being too suspicious.

What I hadn't bargained for was our return trip to Melbourne being on another small plane. I thought I had carefully avoided all those three months ago. Thankfully the winds of yesterday had dropped, the flight smooth enough to ease the hangovers from last night's celebrations. Rest was the order of the day. We have a couple of important dates coming up.

Thursday 5 February

Laurie Brown is now working overtime again. Our main concern is to get Graham Dilley fit for the final matches. Although he has not played for a week there seems little improvement in his shoulder and that is worrying. Chris Broad is also a concern with his hamstring problem. He couldn't field following his innings two days ago.

I had no doubt that Chris would be ready to bat on Sunday in the first final but there was a danger his hamstring might go again, and we could be kept down to ten men in the field. Although Viv Richards had no objection to us using a substitute fielder on Tuesday even though Chris had gone in to the match with the injury, I doubted whether Allan Border would be so generous in the final.

The four days we had spare however did allow Laurie the chance to work on the other aches and strains and I am now looking forward to leading the fittest team I will have had for a month. There was no relaxing now and we were able to organise nets again for the first time since the New Year as well as having regular get-togethers at the hotel.

Friday 6 February

The get-togethers are working and I'm convinced we have come through our shaky period. The qualifying stages of the World Series Cup were rather like the warm-up matches before the Test series started. The matches were a little bit of a drag. Now they are over and the real thing is ahead. The lads just can't wait to get to grips with it. I'm feeling more and more confident each day and so are the rest of the team. Their attitude is simple. Now that we are in the final let's make sure and win it. The grand slam appeals to them.

We will be up against a confident Australian side. They won their fourth match in a row this evening when they beat the West Indies again in Sydney. Viv never made any effort to match the out-of-reach run-rate plus victory he needed to pip us, recognising it was beyond any team. Instead the West Indies – lacking five regulars – just concentrated on a victory, and could not manage that in the end, going down by two wickets.

Saturday 7 February

Graham Dilley is still troubled by his shoulder but we decided this evening that he should play. We will allow him to bowl the ball back from his position in the field, although he must take a chance and hurl it in if there is a run-out opportunity. We also put Phil Edmonds in the 12 and there is a good chance we will go in with two spinners looking at the pitch. We will certainly not be going in as the underdogs – which is how the Australian media now rate us. Again, it is just like the period before the opening Test match when we were written off and Australia billed as certain winners. Their four successive wins seemed to have convinced most people that there was only one team in the final. That suited us. We knew differently, and the team meeting this evening convinced me there would be a few million more throughout Australia who would also know differently by tomorrow evening.

Sunday 8 February

Nothing could have gone sweeter today. An almost flawless performance gave us victory by six wickets with exactly eight overs to spare in the first final in front of 51,000 stunned Australians. You can't have a much healthier win than that.

Everything went right from the time I won the toss after the start had been delayed because of early morning drizzle. The cloudy conditions and a last look at the pitch suggested that it would suit the faster bowlers particularly at the start, so we changed our minds about Phil Edmonds. I needed to win the toss to make sure I had the first chance of bowling and the call was correct.

From that moment on practically everything went our way. Ian Botham with his power and savage hitting assured us of a victory, scoring 71 out of our first 91 runs inside 15 overs. There were no batting shakes this time. We were a little surprised that no effort was made to play the match over the full 50 overs despite starting an hour late. There was no reason why it should have been cut to 44 overs. We did ask the Australian authorities if it were possible to go the full distance, but Peter Lush was told it was not. I guess television planning and schedules ruled again.

Not that I had a thought for anything once the match started. I found myself pretty busy straight away. In the first over from Graham Dilley I held an edge at slip to get rid of Tim Zoehrer who had been promoted to opener after hitting 50 in quick time against the West Indies in that position two days earlier. In Daffy DeFreitas' first over I held another edge to send back Geoff Marsh. The innings was only eight balls old and Australia were three for two.

They were lucky not to be 21 for four. I took another edge, this time from Allan Border, only to hear the no-ball shout against Graham for overstepping as I wrapped my hands around the ball. I was convinced an edged drive from Dean

Ian Botham, Player of the Finals

Jones against Graham was headed straight for my outstretched left hand but somehow it went through for four. I still can't understand how I missed it.

Australia's third-wicket pair did stay around to add 106 but when Neil Foster had Border caught behind off a great delivery, the rest seemed to fold and by the time their 44 overs were up we had limited them to 171 for eight.

It was a sizeable total in the reduced number of overs, but Ian made it seem ridiculous from about the third over onwards when he suddenly produced a searing drive against Simon Davis. From that moment he was in his element: cutting, driving, pulling with his immense strength until off-spinner Greg Matthews had him caught on the long-off boundary. We were 91, he was 71 including one six and 11 fours, Chris Broad was 12 and the match was virtually won.

David Gower sealed it all with 45 runs off only 47 balls, a lovely effort containing some beautifully timed strokes, but everybody was still talking about Ian's innings and he was certainly the toast of our dressing room this evening. It was the start of one or two celebration drinks that evening that finished up in my room with some of the English cricket writers. I have to say they were as pleased as we were.

England v Australia (First Final)
Played at Melbourne, Feb 8

Australia 171 for 8 (44 overs) (D.M. Jones 67)
England 172 for 4 (36 overs) (I.T. Botham 71, D.I. Gower 45)

England won by 6 wickets.

Monday 9 February

Our victory was a shock to the Australian system just as our first Test win in Brisbane had been. The papers made nice reading as we headed off for yet another internal airline trip. There was one more plane ticket left, a return trip to Melbourne for the third final. We were all determined we would not use it; there was the promise of a four-day break awaiting us in Sydney if we could wrap up the World Series Cup at the second meeting. That was a great spur. I think it occupied the thoughts of all of us flying into Sydney. Our next flight out was going to be home.

Tuesday 10 February

Again, our first thoughts had to be abandoned today when we looked at the Sydney pitch. Phil Edmonds had been pencilled in again knowing Sydney's reputation for assisting spin bowlers. That idea was altered when we discovered the pitch had been heavily watered the previous day and was still very damp, so we took the decision this evening to stick with Neil Foster, especially as he had bowled so well against Dean Jones in two games.

We were given a further incentive today to get the finals over quickly. It was announced that Chris Broad had been voted 'International Player of the Year', for which he has won a £16,000 car, the richest individual prize in cricket and one he thoroughly deserves. We were all convinced he would win it, but you never know for certain with some judging panels, the Channel Nine commentators having voted Viv Richards 'Player of the Series' for the qualifying rounds of the World Series Cup. It was an astonishing choice considering the West Indies had failed to qualify and Richards had been outscored by Broad, Geoff Marsh and Dean Jones.

Wednesday 11 February

That's it, all over. The World Series Cup wrapped up in two matches, three trophies in the bag and home on Monday, arguably the most successful touring side of all time. It's party time, too, following our tense eight-run victory, our prize-taking complete when Ian Botham was named 'Player of the Finals'. There was no question of him not deserving it. He had provided us with another blitz start, although much shorter this time, and then nipped in with three wickets which put the skids under the Australian innings. All this with a swollen and damaged left foot that forced him to leave the field immediately he completed his ten overs, although he was reluctant to go.

Again I was fortunate in calling correctly which allowed us to do what we wanted which was to bat first, although the move was not as successful as I had hoped it would be. Still we had the ever-dependable Chris Broad to shore things up with yet another half century which provided the backbone of the innings.

Ian was just getting warmed up, having hit four boundaries, when Greg Ritchie stuck out his right hand at backward square leg and held a ball destined to thump against the boards. That was our first set back. Bill Athey and David Gower stayed

Another half century for Chris Broad

for even less time and the future looked dark when Chris and I were out to successive deliveries. Chris was caught at mid-wicket and I was run out next ball, sent back attempting to run a second. I thought I had just beaten Steve Waugh's return from long leg but a television replay showed Dick French had made a correct decision, although it was so close I could have been given the benefit of the doubt. We then had to rely on Allan Lamb to take us to 187.

It was touch and go, I needed bowling of the highest quality with keen fielding to make it work and I got it. The mood was set before we went out when Graham Dilley asked me to help him have a few looseners. I asked Daffy if he was coming out and he said 'No, I feel okay skip'. But he must have been watching because he appeared after Graham had sent down a couple, walked up to me and commented, 'He's really serious about this one isn't he? I'll be with him'.

A policeman adds light relief at the boundary

173

They were both right on line so that Geoff Marsh and Allan Border were never able to get away, and scored only 18 runs off the first ten overs. It did start to get a little worrying when they got through another nine overs together and began to look menacing. Then Ian struck for the first time, having Border caught behind on the leg side and between the 20th and 30th overs he captured the wickets of Marsh and Greg Ritchie. John Emburey then held a return drive from Dean Jones, throwing himself full length to his left, getting up from the ground without any of the hystrionics Greg Matthews has shown. Even more vital was the fact that Ian and John limited Australia to just 19 runs off those ten overs, and that put the later batsmen under much pressure. I don't think I have seen John bowl so brilliantly in a one-day game – and I've seen him bowl in a lot.

With 74 wanted off the last ten, and then 50 off the last five I always thought we would do it, even when Simon O'Donnell hit two huge sixes against Daffy, who refused to get ruffled by the treatment. Australia needed 18 off the last over to win – the target Allan Lamb had faced on our last visit here against Australia, getting them in five balls.

I brought Neil Foster back to bowl. 'You pick some right times to bring me on', he said. I just wished him luck, told him to pitch it up around leg stump and even O'Donnell couldn't belt him when he got down the other end.

It was all over, the dressing room was alive and I struggled to hold the tears. I'm not quite sure how I got through the television and press interviews and it was not until I got to the barbecue party Elton John threw on the rooftop of our apartment block in Bondi Junction that I was able to relax and take it all in.

It went on all night and I don't think too many of us remember the details, but it is a party I shall remember forever – a party to celebrate a magnificent job well done as well as saying farewell to Australia. Now for British Airways and home!

England v Australia (Second Final)
Played at Sydney, Feb 11

England 187 for 9 (50 overs) (B.C. Broad 53, A.J. Lamb 36)
Australia 179 for 8 (50 overs) (S.R. O'Donnell 40*)

England won by 8 runs.   Man of Finals: I.T. Botham

Simon O'Donnell couldn't quite match Lamb's 18 off the last over

Home thoughts from abroad

By the time we came to file out through Sydney's International Airport after our well-earned three day end-of-tour wind down to complete our four month visit, we left behind one very depressed Australian cricketing nation. Their media seemed preoccupied with the unpalatable thought – for a country that can't abide losers – that Australia must now be considered the wooden spoonists when it comes to rating the standings of the Test playing countries in a league table based on recent results. That, of course, is putting aside Sri Lanka. The latest Test playing country is still not yet considered as part of the 'big league' involving ourselves, India, Pakistan, the West Indies, New Zealand and Australia.

The wooden spoonists tag was the one that the Australian media gleefully threw in our direction when we arrived last October at the same airport terminal building after our defeats at the hands of the West Indies, India and New Zealand over the previous nine months – carefully forgetting that Australia had not exactly set the international cricketing scene alight since they had been thrashed by us during the 1985 summer at home.

We were feeling good at that moment. We were looking good, too. A complete team, well balanced and one where every player knew exactly what he had to do. Yet I was only too well aware that in 12 months' time, everything could be changed again. That is not being pessimistic. It is being a realist although, having started my captaincy period in the doldrums, I hope I never lose another Test series during the length of the time I remain in charge. I never want to taste again the despair I felt during the 1986 summer.

Yet I feel it is only right to point out that there is a greater danger these days of us slipping and losing series people expect us to win even if we play to the best of our ability. Leaving aside series involving the West Indies, most others since the start of the 1980s have been very close. All countries have had periods in that time – some of them short – when they might have had the right to consider themselves the second best Test playing country behind the Caribbean Cavaliers under Clive Lloyd's command. Even India and Pakistan. There was a time when losing to both those countries – and New Zealand – was unthinkable, especially with home advantage. Those days have gone – possibly forever. It is something the cricket watching public have still not wholly accepted. They had better get used to it.

Where is the disgrace in losing to a side containing Richard Hadlee, the Crowe brothers Martin and Jeff, John Wright and led by such a shrewd captain as Jeremy

Coney? He may not be an outstanding international player but he is a deep thinker who knows exactly how to bring out the best in those around him, a Mike Brearley figure in charge. Where is the disgrace in losing to a side containing Sunil Gavaskar, the heaviest scoring batsman in Test history, Kapil Dev, Dilip Vengsarkar and others? There is none as long as we give everything in the attempt. I can assure everybody, we did just that.

There are some who will argue that the fact that there is little to choose between most international sides these days – the West Indies apart – is due to a general levelling down process, the standard of England and Australia having fallen. I don't accept that for one moment, whatever Fred Trueman and others of his playing days may say. I believe there has been a levelling up, the players from the other countries are now far more worldly wise in the ways of Test cricket than they have ever been.

I've already noted earlier in the diary that I don't believe this present West Indies side is over the hill at this moment as some are suggesting. When they still have Gordon Greenidge, Desmond Haynes, Viv Richards and Malcolm Marshall to call upon, it would be stupid to write them off. But the signs are there that their years of complete dominance are coming to an end. With their fast bowling power base, they have had it fairly easy, especially when playing at home, but I am sure they are going to find things a little tougher over the next two years or so. They will find themselves more and more in situations where they will have to fight to get out of trouble and this is where they will have to rely on character as much as pure ability. Other countries should be able to snatch more than just the very occasional victory from them. Perhaps come out even in a five match series.

Their own authorities have started to admit that they are worried about where their next Test batsmen are coming from. Their success at Test level has encouraged the island teams in Caribbean domestic cricket to follow the same formula with attacks based on menacing pace. This, in turn, has hindered the development of their younger batsmen. West Indian batsmen don't like being exposed to non-stop fast bowling any more than any others in the world. Although the West Indies Test side has made the rest of the world suffer by their accent on speed, so their own cricket has apparently suffered likewise. Once Gordon, Desmond, Viv and one or two more decide to call it a day – and their senior players are not getting any younger – the West Indies look as though they could struggle to make runs so giving other countries a greater chance. I don't think they will have difficulty finding fast bowlers for some time to come judging by the number who were queueing up to have a go at us early in 1986 but the threat from pace is likely to become less as other countries start to take action over what they believe is an excessive amount of short pitched fast bowling.

The Australians put forward an attempted fast bowling curb during the International Cricket Conference in 1986 when they produced a paper which suggested that all bouncers should be banned. That, in my opinion, was taking things too far. The right for a fast bowler to bowl a bouncer has to be retained as long as the bowler uses it in the correct way. By that I mean using the delivery as an occasional weapon, a surprise element perhaps when a batsman is beginning to play with some comfort and regularity off the front foot.

Again the Australians have taken more action than other countries in preventing short pitched fast bowling in their one day cricket by introducing a measure which permits the square leg umpire to call 'no ball' for any delivery which goes above shoulder high of a batsman standing normally in the crease. The square leg umpire is probably in a better position to judge than the umpire at the bowler's end and that idea has some merit in it. The West Indies were not happy with the rule when we played against them. I don't think it is the complete answer because much will depend on the umpire standing at square leg. Some are tougher than others in this respect. Yet the very fact that countries are earnestly seeking ways of curbing too much short pitched bowling must make the West Indies think.

There should be further moves at the 1987 International Cricket Conference. The members have been trying for some time to get the West Indies to agree to a minimum number of overs per day in Test matches, bringing them into line with everybody else. So far the West Indies have resisted the proposals. One of their arguments, I gather, is that they often bowl around 90 overs a day because their fast bowlers bowl so many no balls!

I believe the time for talking and gentle persuasion is over. I would hope that either England or Australia – two founder members – would put a firm proposal at the next meeting calling for a minimum number of overs per day in all Test cricket. A resolution which would be seconded and carried so that the West Indies are brought into the same camp as every other country.

Such a move might even prove a benefit to the West Indies. They would certainly have to think about introducing a little more spin into their attack. For instance I know that John Emburey considers Roger Harper one of the finest off spin bowlers in the world. The West Indies clearly believe they have at least one other off spinner just as good in taking Clyde Butts to New Zealand this year instead of Harper. It would be nice to see both in their Test team.

This would all help towards making international cricket even more competitive for the next few years so that no side – even the West Indies – could be fully confident of taking a series. Their fans – like those in England who were used to seeing India, Pakistan and New Zealand seen off with great regularity – would have to accept the fact that their own side has no automatic right to victory however unpleasant that thought may prove.

The game does benefit. It is in a far healthier state financially as a result of the levelling up process that has gone on. English county cricket relies on the end of season cash hand out from the Test and County Cricket Board to keep going. The hand out comes from the money made from the home Test and one day international games from a variety of sources – sponsorship, television fees and money through the turnstiles.

There was a time not so long ago when England hauled in money from a summer visit by Australia and the West Indies and could hand every county organisation a satisfying cash bonanza. In between, however, counties had to tighten their money belts as the hand out was less than half when the other countries were the visitors.

That no longer happens. Recent summers have shown that the increased competitiveness of Pakistan, India and New Zealand has resulted in full house crowds for one day internationals and near sell out crowds on the first three days of Test matches. Twenty years ago those three countries were never considered a drawing card because England were expected to win often one sided matches. Today the cricket fan is attracted because he is pretty sure he is going to see a fiercely contested match.

The remarkable increase in the amount of Test cricket played over the last ten years has been partly responsible for the change. Twenty years ago New Zealand found it difficult to engage opposition, apart from regular visits by England made almost as an afterthought following an England tour of Australia. Even the Australians did not consider New Zealand worth playing. New Zealand's cricketers were desperately lacking in the feeling of Test cricket. India and Pakistan were slightly better off. But not much.

That has all changed. For the last ten or 15 years there has been a regular programme of Test cricket – too much in the opinion of the majority of players in the last five years – so that all players now have the opportunity to become well versed in the requirements needed to be successful. They get regular exposure to crowds, pressure situations, world class bowlers. All that was denied them before.

The move to standardise Test pitches has also been a factor. There are still variations the world over but they are only slight these days with all Test pitches being covered fully the moment a drop of rain falls. No longer do we see overseas batsmen struggling to put bat to ball on a rain affected pitch as they did when Derek Underwood first started in Test cricket. He was even more unplayable then than he is now on a pitch offering him some assistance. It was not surprising England could sweep opposition aside 20 years ago. Unfortunately, too, we have made it harder for ourselves in this country. We are mainly responsible, in my view, for raising the standard of other sides at Test level by throwing open our county dressing room doors and welcoming overseas players into our domestic game.

I appreciate that the move might have been necessary at the time to stimulate the game domestically but it has resulted in English county cricket becoming a training ground for young Test players from overseas. The importation of overseas players went way beyond the original intention, which was to sprinkle county cricket with a few star names. When those star names were used up, counties then started importing completely unknown youngsters of potential. The players arrived, played and then went away to build Test careers and reputations with their own countries – often taking it out on us. Perhaps it says something for the talent spotting ability of county sides, but there have not been too many young unknowns from overseas who have been signed up and then failed to play a Test for their country of birth. I am sure the start of New Zealand's rise as a Test playing power coincided with the entry into county cricket of Geoff Howarth with Surrey, John Wright at Derbyshire, Glen Turner and John Parker with Worcestershire and Richard Hadlee at Notts. They all become better players as a result and were the main constituents of a New Zealand that started taking Test matches from all the other Test playing countries.

The transformation in those players and the confidence they gained from knowing that they had improved, combined with their willingness to work at their game, turned them into big time players capable of holding their own at the highest level.

Even more important was the fact that the other players around them – all part timers in that they held down regular jobs to provide them with a living – began to believe in themselves as New Zealand's success rate increased. They were also helped by a feeling of togetherness and fine team spirit which is an essential ingredient in any winning side, as we proved in Australia. Where they would have crumbled and fallen away in crucial situations of the past, they found new resolve to hang in and fight it out.

Martin Crowe is another outstanding example. He had the look of a very promising batsman about him when I first saw him with New Zealand in England in 1983 but his year with Somerset in 1985 when he deputised for Viv Richards, made all the difference to him. He struggled during the first half of the county season, came good during the second half and looked then the world class batsman he is today.

The New Zealand side of the next few years will obviously be built around him but there must be concern by the New Zealand cricketing authorities about the future health of their Test side, because they are likely to be without players with county cricket experience very shortly. Howarth has already gone, along with Turner and Parker. Wright and Hadlee are reaching the stage when they could announce their retirement from international cricket at any time, while Coney's leadership will be missing at the end of this year. They will still have Martin Crowe as an English cricket educated player and Dipak Patel, the former Worcestershire all rounder who has now settled there. But with the tightening of regulations concerning overseas players in county cricket, they don't appear to have anybody else likely to play in our championship.

There is no greater example of how we in England have helped the West Indies assume all their cricketing power than that shown by the make up of their side over the years. I have no doubt that the team Clive Lloyd led – I should say two teams, for the one at the end of his period in charge was vastly different from the one he inherited in the mid 1970s – would have proved a tremendous force in world cricket if none of the players involved had experienced county cricket. They were extremely rich in natural ability. But, then again, West Indies teams always have been. What they often lacked was patience to go with their flair to make them consistently successful at the highest level. Playing in county cricket gave them that patience and steel, making the likes of Viv Richards, Rohan

Kanhai, Alvin Kallicharran, Andy Roberts, Colin Croft, Joel Garner and a host of others. Now Surrey's Tony Gray looks like taking over where Garner leaves off. He is a fine young bowler in the Garner mould on the verge of making a regular Test place for himself but I wonder whether he would have got this far so quickly if it had not been for Surrey's interest in him at the start of the 1985 summer at home. He appeared from nowhere, made a dramatic start to his county championship life and immediately the West Indies selectors took notice. In my mind there is no doubt that the influence of county cricket on all of them is the main reason why the West Indies were able to cash in on their fast bowling strength and become such a dominating force.

Pakistan have benefited similarly with a number of their younger players following the path trod by Mushtaq Mohammad into county cricket with Northamptonshire. There was his brother Sadiq, Zaheer Abbas, Sarfraz Nawaz, Javed Miandad, Asif Iqbal, Imran Khan, Majid Khan and Intikhab Alam. There are nine names for a start and what a team they would make.

I know that several of them had technical flaws when they first appeared in this country, flaws they would probably have never ironed out if they had stayed in Pakistan because pitches over there never exposed them. They were exposed by county bowlers operating in English conditions. The only way Zaheer and co were able to make a success of their new careers was to work at those shortcomings which, in turn, made them more fitted for Test cricket. Zaheer was very much a one sided player when he first started. By the time he finished with Gloucestershire he could play all around the wicket. English cricket made him.

Indian players have never been so keen to make similar journeys into our cricket although Farokh Engineer had an impressive wicketkeeping-cum-batting career with Lancashire, Kapil Dev has enjoyed himself, and Sunil Gavaskar had a season with Somerset. That was too late to help Gavaskar because he was already a world beater by then but Engineer and Dev were undoubtedly helped and it is interesting that Ravi Shastri – an ambitious young man – has agreed to try his all rounder ability with Glamorgan.

The new restrictions on the number of overseas players a county can field, which will soon reduce every county side to only one non-qualified England player in their first team, will help England's cause by not making the other countries quite so effective. Yet I still feel we are a little too generous in this country, especially when acting as hosts to touring sides. We give them far more assistance then we get when we go abroad.

Those are the reasons why I believe everything has evened up at a world level, why the world standings of Test teams can change dramatically over a six month period. Although the Australian media were lamenting that Allan Border's team were left holding the wooden spoon as a result of our grand slam triumph, things could easily change. They could prove a far tougher side when we face them in a one-off Test match in Sydney early in 1988 to celebrate the country's bi-centenary.

They were an improved side by the end of our visit. Something had got through to them during the one day internationals. I thought they were a little innocent in their approach when they played against us in the Perth Challenge and when I saw them in their other matches in the competition. By the time they approached the finish of the World Series competition, they had got their act together more. Bowlers were being brought on at the right time against the right batsmen – both ours and the West Indies'. It caused us to change our approach when we got to the finals to counter the moves Australia had made. Their field placings were also more realistic. They had obviously been thinking about the game and I suspect Dirk Wellham's inclusion must have had some influence.

They have got the nucleus of a good side, building on Geoff Marsh, a very solid and reliable opening batsman as well as being a very pleasant character. He was a good influence on the side and I began to understand why they made him vice captain although he had very little leadership experience.

Steve Waugh has the makings of a very good batsman. I'm not sure whether he will ever make it as a genuine third seam bowler, the role Australia cast him in against us a couple of times, at a Test level but he is a more than useful one day medium paced bowler.

Bruce Reid, the tall and lean left arm pace bowler from Western Australia – known as the 'walking wicket' to our lads – was most impressive considering his limited first class experience. He is definitely one for the future if he can build on what he has already achieved although he needs help as a wicket-taker for his country at the moment. He is another pleasant personality.

They also have high hopes of Mark Taylor, the stocky, left handed New South Wales opening batsman who has had only two years of first class experience so far. He did not make any impression against us on the wet Newcastle wicket when we played New South Wales in a State match but conditions were against him on that occasion. From what I heard, he could make it. He was the player they were supposed to have selected when they named his New South Wales colleague Peter Taylor, the unknown off spinner, for the fifth and final Test. The way things turned out I think they knew which one they were going for all the time, despite the stories. Peter certainly caused us a few problems. I know John Emburey was quite taken with him. In his particular trade being 30 when making his Test debut was probably a help because he didn't get rattled when we did try to get after him. I'd still like to see him in a Test match on a pitch not helping him as the Sydney pitch did before I made up my mind completely about him but there is potential for Australia to work with.

By the end of the tour Victoria's batsman Dean Jones had become the nation's hero with his flurry of big scores including taking three centuries from us, one in the final Test and two in one day internationals. With the double century he scored in India just prior to our tour to Australia, it is easy to understand why the Australians have got so excited about him. We all still have our doubts about him. Largely, I suppose, because he should have been out before he reached three figures in any of those innings against us. I was the guilty party who allowed him to make his first three figures score in Perth when dropping a catch he offered. He had a charmed life from then on. I think he needs to calm down a little if he is going to be really successful over a period in Test cricket. He gives the bowler a chance. Although he is a fast runner between the wickets he would also frighten me if I were a captain with the unnecessary risks he takes going for singles.

Simon O'Donnell is another chancy player as a batsman and I saw several in that mould when playing against their State sides, batsmen who appeared to be in too much of a hurry. Nice, clean strikers of the ball, hitting it a long way yet who have not learned which deliveries to have a go at and which ones to leave alone. They need to be more patient.

But there is material for Bobby Simpson to work on and a chance yet that Allan Border could get the help he needs to prove a series winner as a captain.

I'm just glad he didn't turn the corner in that respect against us and would like to take this chance to thank him for a good, clean fight in a series that never boiled over despite a number of tense situations when each side was jockeying for control. I'd like to pay a tribute to our lads while on that point. I thought their behaviour on the field was a credit to them and their country. Not once did I have to hand out a lecture in that respect and that is unusual in this age.

In retrospect

With the feel of English soil under my feet once more it is time to come down to earth after all the heady stuff in Australia. It's not going to be easy. For some time now I know I shall be reliving the triumphs and the magic of 'down under' all over again whenever I meet relatives and friends who will want to share in the stories and taste the experience.

The reception on our return has been astonishing. We sensed from 12,000 miles away that our performances had captured the imagination at home and I know the regular cricket writing group travelling the distance with us felt as shattered mentally and physically as we did towards the end of the tour with the hours they put in writing extra stories after our victories. We felt, too, the disappointment when it looked as though we had blown our chances of reaching the finals of the World Series Cup and the folk at home were wondering what had happened to us.

There have been the odd cynics who have said we beat a poor Australian side, were fortunate to meet the West Indies when they were suffering injury problems, and should have beaten Pakistan anyway in the Perth Challenge. I treat them with contempt, regard them as jealous knockers who will find fault in any triumph.

I admit we were helped a little by a couple of strange selection decisions which, perhaps, denied Allan Border his best XI in a couple of Test matches. But that did not make them a bad side. They tried hard, worked studiously at their game under their cricket manager Bobby Simpson, gave their all. It wasn't good enough simply because we never gave them the chance to be good enough. It was as simple as that: to beat any international side on their home ground has got to be a triumph.

As for the West Indies, they still proved to be a fearsome bowling force. It was their batting that let them down – again because our bowlers were too good for them in the conditions. Certainly they had a look of frailty about them that suggests that there is light at the end of the tunnel for the other nations challenging for supremacy in the cricket world. Moreover if other nations were to adopt the firm policy of the Australian board in Test matches we might be in for some very open cricket. I know they missed some of their star players from match to match. All I can say about that is that I'm proud of the way our players kept going when they were suffering from hamstring strains and the like. The Pakistan jibe is nonsense, too. With the exception of the West Indies in the Caribbean, no side can expect to beat another automatically these days and Pakistan had knocked over the West

Indies and Australia before we scuttled them twice. Yes, magic moments, all of which deserve the accolades that have been heaped on the team. But it is time to take stock. The new season at home is not far off, just time for a breather. That is the way of cricket these days. With what promises to be a fascinating series against Pakistan ahead, we can't afford to get carried away.

We must not fall into the danger of trying to live off Australian memories alone. We have to build on what we have achieved, shape the side for the coming Test series and look beyond to the World Cup in India and Pakistan next October and the tours of Pakistan and New Zealand that follow when we will be without Ian Botham. And, I suspect, David Gower as well.

The main concern must centre around Beefy. He has announced he will never tour with England, settling for life with Queensland instead in-between seasons at home. I have no doubt that some people will argue that he should never be picked for England again in our summers, although he is still keen to play for his country at home, for he does appreciate he needs Test cricket to keep his name alive.

My own thoughts on that subject are very clear. If I am invited to captain England this summer against Pakistan I shall do everything in my power to make sure that he gets in the side, provided he is in form for his new county, Worcestershire. I have little doubt that he will be.

But, before pleading his case, I shall ask for the same commitment he showed on the Australian trip. By that I mean a willingness to run in and bowl aggressively off his full distance so that he is capable of playing the full all-rounder role, and not be content with bowling the medium-paced variety he was forced to resort to in Australia following his strained rib injury.

Without playing the role of a genuine third seamer we would have to find another bowler to slip into the Test side which would, in turn, mean leaving out one of the spinners, and thereby interfering with the whole balance of the team. I would not want to do that. I prefer to have two spin bowlers available unless the pitch conditions argue against it.

I have heard it suggested by people in many quarters that Ian's England future in international cricket lies as a batsman who could bowl a little. A future as a number five batsman, allowing room for a genuine all-rounder in the normal six position. I would rather see him as the all-rounder, not a pure batsman. I know he has made almost 5,000 Test runs from his 89 Test matches and hit 14 centuries but I have to be honest and say he would certainly have to be more consistent if he was to score the number of runs expected regularly from a number four or five batsman. His whole approach to cricket is suited to the all-rounder role, a person who wants to be involved in every facet of the game. I think he needs that role, for Ian likes to know that if he does fail with the bat he always has the chance to make amends with the ball, or vice versa.

I hope he tells me he intends to bowl off his full run again when I have a word with him because we still need him. He was a marvellous asset in Australia, true to his word in every way when he promised before the tour that he would remain fully committed and turned on. Looking back, I don't think I could have asked much more of him both on and off the field. He set up the first Test victory for us in Brisbane with that hard-hitting century and finished the tour in a blaze in the final matches of the World Series Cup. He attended every fielding and net session he was asked to and produced more than a few words at team meetings that got the rest of the lads in the mood. He was never short of advice on the field either.

For me that was one of the fascinating parts of the tour—working so closely with Ian, David Gower and John Emburey. Listening to their thoughts, views and tactical appreciation before deciding on the policy to adopt. That helped make us winners. Between us, and with Micky Stewart, we analysed the game of every Australian batsman we came across and were able to set the appropriate field for them in the one-day internationals, cutting off their best scoring strokes. There was not one match where the opposition scored the number of runs they should have done in the conditions. We were always able to hold them in check. To be able to do that requires the co-operation of the bowlers in bowling the right line consistently. Or bowling in the channel as Micky called it. He never stopped telling them, and I don't think I have ever played with such a well disciplined attack. It was a great thrill to be able to stand at slip to Graham Dilley and Phil DeFreitas in the end, watching them work so accurately. It got to the stage where we just knew they were going to make a breakthrough in the opening spell.

Graham has returned home a truly world-class strike bowler. He bowls from closer to the wicket than he used to three or four years ago, is more sideways on and swings the ball away magnificently from the right hander at full pace. After dropping that skier from Allan Border in the Adelaide one-day international which made the going tougher for us to reach the finals, he did suffer a little drop in confidence and allowed his shoulder injury to bother him when he might have been able to ignore it. But once we got him bowling again in a match, his confidence returned and I can envisage three or four wonderful years ahead for him, although I don't think there will be too many opening batsmen who will be appreciating his skill in Test matches from now on.

By the end of the tour Daffy had formed an ideal opening partner for Graham with his pace and his movement off the wicket, the styles of each complimenting the other. I think you have to go back to Ian Botham's early years in Test cricket when he joined Bob Willis to find a partnership that was so good. Daffy never failed to surprise me. His performance on the tour for a 20-year-old was almost unbelievable and he finished with an extremely old and wise head on his young shoulders. Ian Botham took a close interest in him and taught him a lot and it was Daffy's capacity for listening and then putting into practice the advice he had been given which impressed me. He needs to work a little more on his batting now when he returns to Leicestershire. He didn't quite make the weight of runs I thought he might after opening with 40 in the First Test in Brisbane, but everything else he did showed vast improvement. I never had to worry whenever the ball went in the air in Daffy's direction. I knew he would catch it. His fielding was an inspiration for the rest of us, his returns leaving the wicket-keeper with little to do especially if there was a chance of a run-out.

Daffy is arguably the most exciting young player in the world now, yet at the start of the tour he was virtually an unknown. He is level-headed enough to make his rich ability count. Only time will tell whether he can improve his batting to the point where he can fully take over Ian Botham's number six position in the side. I hope so. If that proves beyond him, he should finish up at number seven.

I can't speak too highly of the other bowlers either. The way Gladstone Small slotted in when we needed him for the Fourth Test in Melbourne when the Ashes were retained and in the Fifth in Sydney. In each match he emerged with five wickets in Australia's first innings. Neil Foster, too, was like a breath of fresh air when he got his chance in the World Series Cup competition. He was not too happy when he failed to make the Test side in a couple of matches when he thought he had a chance. He can get quite angry, but I would sooner have somebody like that in my squad than a player who just shrugs his shoulders and shows no disappointment when his name is not on the team sheet. Fozzy never once allowed his disappointment to affect his attitude, working hard in the nets ready to grab that chance when it came.

One of the most satisfying aspects of the tour was seeing spinners John Emburey and Phil Edmonds prove that their species still has a huge part to play in Test cricket in an age when fast bowlers fill most bowling positions. John certainly enjoyed himself and I enjoyed watching him. He inspired the Australians to use two spinners in the end, even in one-day games, something the Australians have been reluctant to do in the past when they have preferred a succession of medium-paced bowlers. John proved beyond doubt, in my opinion, that he is the number one off spinner in the world and did away with the suspicion that he can't run through a side by his performances in Brisbane in the First Test and Sydney in the final game. Phil was not quite so successful in wicket-taking terms yet helped us establish control when we needed it and will no doubt be telling everybody throughout the summer that we should have played him more often.

If I expected both of them to play a leading role in the Ashes' battles, I certainly hoped that Chris Broad would do well also. I was confident he would when I helped select the tour party back in September, but I never expected him to be such an outstanding success throughout the entire tour, overshadowing every other batsman.

His remarkable run – including those three centuries in successive Test matches – led to a change of nickname. He started the tour being known as 'Jessie' but after that third Test century in Melbourne he became known as 'Whoda'. That stood for 'Who would have thought when the tour started that Chris Broad would emerge as England's leading batsman!'

He was astonishing. The longer the tour went on, the hungrier he became for runs, even when he was handicapped by a strained hamstring during the one-day series. There was nothing that would stop him getting to the crease where he stands so tall, solid and defiant. He looks like a left-handed version of Graham Gooch these days and I can think of no higher compliment. Like Graham, he is very strong off his legs and drives powerfully but is selective in the deliveries he wants to hit. The thought of the pair of them opening up for England against Pakistan this summer thrills me as it should thrill every England fan. That may sound a little unfair on Bill Athey whose contribution to our success may have been overlooked in the face of Chris Broad's heroic deeds and the form of our bowlers in the one-day competitions. Yet Bill played a key role in the retention of the Ashes, the winning of the Perth Challenge and the World Series Cup.

He cheerfully accepted the opening role although it meant playing out of position, helping to give our innings the solid starts which provided the platform for big scores early on. I thought he was desperately unlucky not to finish the tour with at least two Test centuries which would have set up his immediate Test future. I see him more as a number three, his Gloucestershire role, rather than an opening batsman and I think he would be happier there. His success in the one-day competitions came from his superb fielding and catching inside the circle. He took some beauties and also cut off many runs through his ground fielding. I know there was some media suggestion that we should drop Bill because he is not a great one for quick scoring, but he was always worth a one-day place in my book.

David Gower surprised me. I should imagine that he surprised a number of other people as well. It is remarkable how many times in the past couple of years or so that David has made the headlines over his batting, those headlines have been accompanied by stories suggesting he is a fading star. He then ends up among the top two in the Test averages.

It happened in the West Indies last winter, yet he was the batsman in form at the end when most of the others had fallen away. It happened at home last summer, but there didn't seem to be anything wrong with his batting when he made 70 at Trent Bridge, and then a century in the final Test at The Oval against New Zealand. It happened on this tour, but when the Ashes series was over, there he was second in the averages behind Chris Broad, his average over 50, as well as being the second highest run scorer.

I have to admit I too was a little worried about him as the First Test approached, but once he got into the big time again it was all there when we needed it. He has the ability to turn it on when it matters, and you have to learn to ignore his form and returns in the other games. There are some – indeed many – batsmen who would not be able to succeed on that approach but David has been around a long time now. Just one net session with the ball moving sweetly off his bat can set him up as it did in Perth for the Second Test match. He probably has to reserve his big efforts for the important occasions now after non-stop cricket for the last ten years. Because I wonder just how much longer David can keep going at this pace. This is one reason why I wouldn't be surprised to see him take this next winter off, away from touring Pakistan and New Zealand, so that he can have a well-deserved break. If he did he could run the risk of losing his Test place the following summer. But I don't think that it is such a big risk in his case. A winter off would bring him back fresher, renew his enthusiasm and might even prolong his Test career for another three or four years to England's great benefit.

The disadvantage of taking a winter off is losing all Test and touring income;

this seems unfair as David has given so much to the game in every way. That is one reason why I want to have talks with the Test and County Cricket Board this summer to see if there could be some form of compensation in such cases.

I would also like to have talks about some form of bonus scheme for Test cricketers based on the number of Test matches played, similar to the one the Australians operate. With the growing demands on players, in the shape of extra Tests and one-day internationals, I believe it is only right now that some sort of insurance plan should be worked out. On top of the Test match fee, each player should have a sum invested by the TCCB for every Test he plays over ten games, the money being paid back to the player with the interest after he has retired from first-class cricket. The player himself could bump up the final settlement figure by investing part of his Test match fee as well.

One of the greatest moments for me on the tour was being able to tell Bruce French he was playing for his country again towards the end of the World Series Cup competition. Very little went right for Bruce during the first three months of the tour. Our poor batting returns in the opening games made it essential we turned to Jack Richards in the Test matches and he did everything we asked of him. He did more in a way, forced to keep wicket in Tasmania when Bruce fell ill; Jack had not had any rest at all when it came to the one-day tournament. By then he had also suffered a 'flu attack which left him feeling under the weather, giving Bruce his chance to come in when we started to flag a little. Like Neil Foster, Bruce had continued to work hard in the nets and he was as sharp as ever when he got behind the wicket again despite not having played for almost two months. I was very happy for him.

There were disappointments on the tour and I suppose Wilf Slack was the biggest one, especially as I had pushed for his selection in the first place. He never really came to terms with the conditions during the warm-up period and once Chris and Bill established themselves, there was no way in for Wilf, although I still regard him as one of the finest opening batsmen in England.

Allan Lamb was another disappointment in the Test series with a top score of only 46. I found this rather puzzling because as he has proved in the past he has so much ability and I thought the Australian conditions would have suited him better than anybody else. It is a long time now, back in 1985 against Sri Lanka at Lord's, since Allan has scored a Test century and he has still not scored one overseas although he has had the luxury of a settled place in the middle order. He will obviously be under pressure this summer although he revelled in the greater freedom of the one-day game, playing superbly in the Perth Challenge when he proved one of the reasons for us getting to the final, particularly in the qualifying game against the West Indies. During the World Series Cup Allan's timing was not quite so good, too often finding the fielders, although he still made valuable contributions whenever he avoided being run out! On three or four occasions we were very close to bringing James Whitaker into the side and I returned home deeply regretting that James never had a chance to show what he could do above playing in the Third Test in Adelaide when he had just one innings.

It is amazing how luck runs. James started the tour better known than his Leicestershire colleague Phil DeFreitas, but Daffy is the one who returned home finding he was being talked about by most people in cricket. I don't think James will be far behind, however. I will back him to be an England player before long. Everybody made a contribution and I regard the whole tour as a success for 16 people and not just 12 or 13. It was a very happy tour as well and my feeling at the start of the journey that we had the right mix turned out to be correct. It was helped by winning, of course, but even if things had gone wrong I still think the mix would have stopped the whole thing falling apart. Micky Stewart had a large part to play in that and I am glad that the spring meeting of the TCCB did the right thing and made him England's full-time cricket manager.

He got the right response from everybody and although I thought he might have had a tendency to be a little sergeant-majorish with the younger players, I suppose that is not a bad thing from time to time. His role will, of course, be different at home, mainly in the search and find category, looking for the next players to come into the England side so that we have the right cover for every position, newcomers who are brought up with the right habits.

Personally, in the end, I didn't find it the ordeal I thought I might have done. Winning made it that much easier, of course, so I was not exposed to the searching questions that were asked of Allan Border by Australian cricket writers trying to explain away defeat. Certainly I think that keeping the wolves at bay was a tough job for Allan and at times the understandable desire to renew national pride spilled over into frustration on the cricket field. There was not quite the harmony between the teams that existed in 1985. Once or twice I was forced to block direct questions from a couple of journalists where the only answer I could have given would have resulted in criticism of the team as a whole or the performance of a player on the odd bad day. I certainly wasn't going to knock the team in public beyond a generalisation when the batting did fail in the one-day games. I don't think that is the way for a captain to behave. Nor do I think it is the captain's position to criticise the umpires. Both sides received some rough decisions in the series but on balance I reckon they evened out. The umpire's job is a very difficult one, made no easier by the giant replay screens, highlighting any error he might make. If these screens are to remain in use – and I would rather see them banished from cricket grounds – it seems crazy that the umpire cannot benefit and consult the replay before making his decision, as is done in American football.

Generally the relationship with the cricket writers went smoothly and I have manager Peter Lush to thank for that in the way it was all organised so that the one side of touring I was apprehensive about posed few problems.

My one other concern at the start of the tour was playing it all in such a way that I gained the respect of the others around me, remembering that I had not had any real success as an England captain up to that point. I believe I succeeded in that objective. I hope I did anyway and I'd like to place on record my sincere thanks to every member of the touring party for making the whole thing so worthwhile. I think I'll do it again. Provided I'm asked, of course.

FINAL TEST AVERAGES: ENGLAND

	M	I	NO	HS	Runs	Avge	100	50	Ct/St
B.C. Broad	5	9	2	162	487	69.57	3	–	5
D.I. Gower	5	8	1	136	404	57.71	1	2	1
M.W. Gatting	5	9	–	100	393	43.66	1	3	5
C.J. Richards	5	7	–	133	264	37.71	1	–	15/1
J.E. Emburey	5	7	2	69	179	35.80	–	1	3
C.W.J. Athey	5	9	–	96	303	33.66	–	3	3
I.T. Botham	4	6	–	138	189	31.50	1	–	10
P.A.J. DeFreitas	4	5	1	40	77	19.25	–	–	1
A.J. Lamb	5	9	1	43	144	18.00	–	–	6
G.C. Small	2	3	1	21*	35	17.50	–	–	1
P.H. Edmonds	5	5	1	19	44	11.00	–	–	2
G.R. Dilley	4	4	2	4*	6	3.00	–	–	1

Also batted: J.J. Whitaker (1 match) 11 (1 ct).

	O	M	Runs	Wkts	Avge	BB	5wI	10wM
G.C. Small	78.4	23	180	12	15.00	5-48	2	–
G.R. Dilley	176.1	38	511	16	31.93	5-68	1	–
I.T. Botham	106.2	24	296	9	32.88	5-41	1	–
P.H. Edmonds	261.4	78	538	15	35.86	3-45	–	–
J.E. Emburey	315.5	86	663	18	36.83	7-87	2	–
P.A.J. DeFreitas	141.4	24	446	9	49.55	3-62	–	–

Also bowled: M.W. Gatting 23-7-39-0; A.J. Lamb 1-1-0-0.

FINAL TEST AVERAGES: AUSTRALIA

	M	I	NO	HS	Runs	Avge	100	50	Ct/St
D.M. Jones	5	10	1	184*	511	56.77	1	3	1
G.R.J. Matthews	4	7	3	73*	215	53.75	–	2	6
A.R. Border	5	10	1	100*	473	52.55	2	1	4
S.R. Waugh	5	8	1	79*	310	44.28	–	3	8
G.R. Marsh	5	10	–	110	429	42.90	1	2	5
G.M. Ritchie	4	8	2	46*	244	40.66	–	–	1
D.C. Boon	4	8	–	103	144	18.00	1	–	1
T.J. Zoehrer	4	7	1	38	102	17.00	–	–	10/-
C.D. Matthews	2	3	–	11	21	7.00	–	–	1
P.R. Sleep	3	4	–	10	25	6.25	–	–	1
M.G. Hughes	4	6	–	16	31	5.16	–	–	2
B.A. Reid	5	7	4	4	14	4.66	–	–	–

Also batted: G.F. Lawson (1 match) 13 (1 ct); C.J. McDermott (1 match) 0, 1 (1 ct)
P.L. Taylor (1 match) 11, 42; D.M. Wellham (1 match) 17, 1 (3 ct).
G.C. Dyer played in one match and did not bat. (2 ct.).

	O	M	Runs	Wkts	Avge	BB	5wI	10wM
P.L. Taylor	55	17	154	8	19.25	6-78	1	–
B.A. Reid	198.4	44	527	20	26.35	4-78	–	–
P.R. Sleep	136	43	316	10	31.60	5-72	1	–
S.R. Waugh	108.3	26	336	10	33.60	5-69	1	–
C.D. Matthews	70.1	14	233	6	38.83	3-95	–	–
M.G. Hughes	136.3	26	444	10	44.40	3-134	–	–

Also bowled: A.R. Border 16-6-32-1; G.F. Lawson 50-9-170-0;
C.J. McDermott 26.5-4-83-4; G.R.J. Matthews 83-11-295-2.

FINAL TOUR AVERAGES

	M	I	NO	HS	Runs	Avge	100	50	Ct/St
N.A. Foster	4	6	2	74*	172	43.00	–	1	4
B.C. Broad	10	18	2	162	679	42.43	3	1	7
I.T. Botham	8	14	2	138	481	40.08	1	2	11
B.N. French	3	5	2	58	113	37.66	–	1	9/1
D.I. Gower	9	16	2	136	508	36.28	1	2	4
A.J. Lamb	10	18	1	105	534	31.41	1	3	11
J.J. Whitaker	5	7	–	108	214	30.57	1	–	1
M.W. Gatting	10	18	–	100	520	28.88	1	3	11
C.W.J. Athey	9	16	1	96	422	28.13	–	4	7
C.J. Richards	9	14	1	133	335	25.76	1	–	26/3
J.E. Emburey	9	14	3	69	279	25.36	–	1	6
W.N. Slack	5	9	–	89	184	20.44	–	1	5
P.A.J. DeFreitas	7	10	2	40	130	16.25	–	–	1
G.R. Dilley	6	6	3	32	39	13.00	–	–	1
G.C. Small	8	11	3	26	100	12.50	–	–	4
P.H. Edmonds	9	10	2	27	95	11.87	–	–	7

	O	M	Runs	Wkts	Avge	BB	5wI	10wM
G.C. Small	258.4	72	626	33	18.96	5-48	3	–
M.W. Gatting	92	27	195	9	21.66	4-31	–	–
N.A. Foster	149	40	352	16	22.00	4-20	–	–
I.T. Botham	182.1	41	496	18	27.55	5-41	1	–
G.R. Dilley	231.1	44	685	21	32.61	5-68	1	–
J.E. Emburey	463.5	131	1023	31	33.00	7-78	3	–
P.A.J. DeFreitas	239	43	754	22	34.27	4-44	–	–
P.H. Edmonds	428.4	122	929	25	37.16	3-37	–	–

Also bowled: C.W.J. Athey 4-0-25-0; A.J. Lamb 1-1-0-0.